Explorations

Graham Foundation / Princeton Architectural Press series

New Voices in Architecture
presents first monographs on emerging designers from around the world

An Architecture of the Ozarks: The Works of Marlon Blackwell

ARO: Architecture Research Office

Charles Rose, Architect

Julie Snow Architects

Leven Betts: Pattern Recognition

Lewis.Tsurumaki.Lewis: Opportunistic Architecture

Plain Modern: The Architecture of Brian MacKay-Lyons

Rick Joy: Desert Works

Think/Make: Della Valle Bernheimer

VJAA: Vincent James Associates Architects

Explorations

The Architecture of John Ronan

Foreword by Toshiko Mori

Graham Foundation for Advanced Studies in the Fine Arts
Chicago

Princeton Architectural Press
New York

Graham Foundation / Princeton Architectural Press

New Voices in Architecture

presents first monographs on emerging designers from around the world

can

Published by
Princeton Architectural Press
37 East Seventh Street
New York, New York 10003

For a free catalog of books, call 1.800.722.6657.
Visit our website at www.papress.com.

Editor: Laurie Manfra
Designer: Jan Haux

Special thanks to: Nettie Aljian, Bree Anne Apperley, Sara Bader,
Nicola Bednarek, Janet Behning, Becca Casbon, Carina Cha, Penny
(Yuen Pik) Chu, Carolyn Deuschle, Russell Fernandez, Pete Fitzpatrick,
Wendy Fuller, Clare Jacobson, Erin Kim, Aileen Kwun, Linda Lee,
John Myers, Katharine Myers, Dan Simon, Andrew Stepanian,
Katie Stokien, Jennifer Thompson, Paul Wagner, Joseph Weston, and
Deb Wood of Princeton Architectural Press
—Kevin C. Lippert, publisher

Library of Congress Cataloging-in-Publication Data
Ronan, John, 1963–
Explorations : the architecture of John Ronan. — 1st ed.
    p.   cm. — (Graham Foundation/PA Press: New voices in architecture)
 Includes bibliographical references.
ISBN 978-1-56898-876-4 (alk. paper)
1. Ronan, John, 1963– 2. John Ronan Architects. 3. Architecture—
United States—History—20th century. 4. Architecture—United States—
History—21st century. I. Title. II. Title: Architecture of John Ronan.
NA737.R594A4 2010
720.92—dc22
                                                    2009024987

Contents

Foreword

In John Ronan's work there is a rare combination of rationality and poetry. His logical and systematic process reflects the long tradition of technical pragmatism that is attributed to the Chicago School of Architecture. In addition to this rational functionalism, his work is infused with a rich sensibility, one that offers a lightness both in its physicality and in the phenomenological experience of it. Chicago has long been a source of influential architects, such as Louis Sullivan and Frank Lloyd Wright, whose work altered the European modernist language. Continuing in this legacy, John's work evolves these inflections, reinterpretations, and inventions in our contemporary society. His work is fresh and playful, despite a clear rigor and discipline applied throughout the design and its execution. Color, texture, surface, and a generous sense of proportion lift the work above a tough and sensible architectural strategy.

Chicago is a gritty industrial city by origin with a complicated political history, but in 2008 we witnessed an overwhelming sense of hope and ambition rise out of it on a global scale. I cannot help but relate John's personal cool, eternal optimism, commitment to social agenda, and elegant manner to that of our current president.

In January 2009, prominent civic leader Valerie Jarrett introduced the new president to the global audience at the World Economic Forum in Davos, Switzerland, by describing Chicago as the place where the new American ethos is based. She talked about the simple, universal values that the city represents: pragmatism, hard work, steadiness, and reliability. She spoke about the diversity and vibrancy of the demographic, saying, "Chicago is a city of opportunity. It remains a place where somebody can arrive with nothing but talent, drive, and a dream, and create a life for themselves and their family…Chicago is a city of hope. A city carved out of the wilderness, a symbol to our nation of what we can build together, if we are willing to work together."[1] Political figures may come and go, but John's work has been etched into the city. It manifests the optimism and hope of a creative individual in a democratic society. The monograph being produced at this particular time in history represents an essential, singular voice from Chicago.

There is a sense of sobriety in John's rigorous analysis of each project—a precise observation of the facts, program, and context. From this foundation, his imagination emerges as his ideas exceed any perceived limits or constraints. His work is often described as minimalist, but there is a fine line between Miesian aesthetics and an obsession with details that make many projects fall static. Instead, the spaces John creates are dynamic. His work is about spatial continuity, experience, and a visceral engagement with materiality. It is, at once, abstract and sensuous.

My strongest impression of John Ronan, as an architect, was at the final presentation for the Perth Amboy High School competition. While other architects had brought a large team of experts, he stood alone. He spoke quietly and clearly and won the hearts of the jury and the public. He is an architect who embodies a deep sense of eminence, as described by Louis Sullivan in *Kindergarten Chats*:

Such [a] man must have both vision and sympathy; within his spirit must reside the powers of worker, inquirer, thinker, dreamer, prophet; of artist, philosopher, metaphysician—which, all, in condensation, shall organize and propel the utterance of the world's great POET—yet to come. Of such is true eminence.[2]

—Toshiko Mori, Robert P. Hubbard Professor in the Practice of Architecture, Harvard University Graduate School of Design

1 Valerie Jarrett, "Presidential Senior Advisor Valerie Jarrett Speaks at World Economic Forum WEF," January 29, 2009, http://bern.usembassy.gov/event_01292009.html.

2 Louis H. Sullivan, *Kindergarten Chats* (New York: Dover Publications, 1979), 106. *Kindergarten Chats* was first published in 1901–2.

Robert McAnulty (RM): Why don't we start with the obligatory Mies question: For many years, Chicago modernists, presumed to be followers of Mies, have struggled with the anxiety of his influence. It would be easy to mistake your work for a continuation of the Miesian tradition, but you claim to have "moved beyond" Mies. Why?

John Ronan (JR): First of all, I see my work in terms of continuity with the modernist past, not a break from it, and I have no anxiety about Mies or Miesian influences. I think of Mies's work like an onion made up of many fine layers, and interesting on many different levels, which is why the work is still relevant today, I suppose. Because it is so rich, there are not many architects who escape its influence, particularly in Chicago. For example, when I worked with Krueck + Sexton in the early nineties, they were working within what I would call Miesian mannerism, playing with the rules and so on, and in some ways the complex formal manipulations of certain architects practicing today can be viewed as the baroque period of this tradition. But I'm not sure that the formal aspects are the most important part of the work, at least for me. Yes, my work is formally similar to Mies, but I see this more as a reflection of where I practice. Chicago, let's face it, is a city of boxes. More important to me are the approaches to space and materiality, which, I think, are still relevant today. Mies's work was very much about refinement more than invention, and we often take a Miesian approach to certain problems; that is, taking a material or constructional system as a given and asking the question: what can we do with this? The elementary school I designed in Hyde Park is an example of this approach. But certain aspects of the work are not relevant today or seem naive, such as the concept of universal space. I am more interested in spaces that can actively adapt to different conditions, as opposed to a more neutral, passive approach as embodied in Mies's work. Also, I am more interested in the experiential quality of perceiving multiple spaces at one time. Other aspects of his work seem out of date now; for instance, there is a certain purity in the work of Mies that does not seem appropriate to our time, and there is also the relationship of the building to the ground, which is being explored in different ways now.

RM: Looking beyond Chicago and Mies, your interest in minimalist geometries and your fascination with surface and materiality recall the early work of Herzog & de Meuron (HdM). Are you more comfortable with being understood in the context of HdM or Kazuyo Sejima of SANAA? Are there others you would add?

JR: I would probably add David Chipperfield and Peter Zumthor to that list. HdM's work, in particular their early work where the building is a direct consequence of the construction, was influential for me. Those projects had the unique quality of being conventional yet at the same time very strange. I remember discussing their early projects with a friend of mine from Chicago, and he just shrugged and said something to the effect of "What's the big deal, it looks like the stuff they were doing at IIT twenty years ago!" At the time, it was incredibly fresh, and there was a clarity and originality to the work that was unlike anything else going on. And of course, the investigation of materiality in their recent projects is something I really admire and try to encourage in my own office. Sejima's work is also very important to me but for different reasons. I am interested in the exploration of space in her work, specifically in the way she translates a simple building diagram into something spatially complex, as well as her experimentation with the relationship between building and landscape. I think her work is perhaps the most original and interesting of that which is directly traceable to Mies, and I was disappointed when she wasn't awarded the commission to design the student center at IIT.

RM: So much of your work is grounded in the formal language of the bar—elongated rectangular volumes, typically one or two stories. One example, the Perth Amboy High School, is composed of a series of parallel bars that slip and slide past one another along their long sides. Although the vocabulary is grounded in the repetition of a simple form, you take pains to ensure that the bars always remain legible as independent figures. Why is that important to you?

JR: In the Perth Amboy project, I was after something formally simple but spatially complex. I can't say that the legibility of the bars was as important as the resulting spatial condition. Slipping the bars in plan created spaces between and around the bars; slipping them in section allowed for a more complex spatial condition in which natural light comes in from different, unpredictable locations. By creating a multitude of bars and staggering them in plan and section, a continuous spatial field formed that also suppressed the legibility of the six academies that constitute the school. This was a deliberate move. The competition brief was written, I felt, in a leading way that suggested six discrete forms for the six different academies, so I knew most of the schemes would do this. I purposely did the opposite.

RM: Can you speak more generally about your formal sensibility? More specifically, why the predominance of rectangular volumes?

JR: I think there are two types of architects. The first designs a form and then at some point in the process says, "Okay, how do I make this form stand up?" Another type starts with a constructional system and says, "What can I do with this?" The form is more or less derivative of the constructional system. My way of working is consistent with the latter type. I start with a system and then try to see what is possible by stretching the limits of that system. The chapel projects are obvious examples of this approach—accepting a certain type of structural material as a given and then exploring its possibilities. For instance, the width of the Chapel in the Woods was determined by the largest Parallam beam available at that time, and that set the proportions for the entire project. Other materials, such as the stressed-skin panels and oriented strand board, were also rectangular and lent themselves to a building more rectilinear in form. In the Precast Chapel, which was all about off-the-shelf precast concrete elements, the tees were staggered to allow light to bounce into the sanctuary, but it is obvious how the form is derivative of the structural system. As another example, the classroom volumes of the Perth Amboy High School sit on a platform on precast double tees determined by the parking requirements—they could span sixty feet (eighteen meters) and were fireproof. The classroom volumes on top correspond to this platform.

RM: In discussing the Perth Amboy High School project, you call the site a Mat and the buildings a Barscape. How does your scheme move beyond the superimposition of a series of bars on a flattened site-plane? More generally, how does landscape figure in your urban projects?

JR: The term *Barscape* was used to identify the bars as one consolidated entity. The Perth Amboy site was not flat; it was high at either end, then sloped down to a large, flat area in the middle, so the bars are not merely superimposed over the site, but calibrated with it, allowing entry at grade from either end on the main level and forming a suspended condition in the middle of the site, under which parking was located. The Towers pierced the Barscape so that they could be entered from parking level at grade, which was critical to the scheme; they were designed to function independently of the school. The site was seen as a continuous Mat programmed for different activities: sports fields at one end, social spaces at the other, and so on. This is, perhaps, typical of how landscape is treated in my other urban projects, as an extension of the building. For example, in the Gary Comer Youth Center, the parking lot where the Drill Team practices its parade routines is directly related to the gymnasium space, where it practices its stage routines. You can look from the street, through the entire building, and out to the parking lot on the other side. I think it is important for the building and the landscape to participate in some kind of dialogue, though the nature of that dialogue changes from project to project.

In the Poetry Foundation, the building actively creates a garden and incorporates the landscape into the building as if it were another room. In this instance, building and landscape are inextricably tied to one another; one is not dominant and the other recessive.

RM: In your writing there are various formulations of the idea that design is a process: "design is a journey, not a product." The end of that journey is a "distillation of forces," the "result of an evolutionary process." It's not so easy to see these projects as the result of a process that is truly open-ended or exploratory. For better or worse, there is a pretty consistent formal sensibility at work. The projects appear as variations on a few formal themes. You're obviously not Peter Eisenman, who said, "Let the process determine the form." It certainly looks like you have an idea where you're going before you start moving. So why all the talk about process? How does it come through in the work?

JR: Well, first of all, I would say that my design process is basically intuitive, and while the resulting formal characteristics might be similar from project to project, the design strategy employed is not. For instance, in designing the Poetry Foundation, I looked at a dozen different strategies for combining a garden with a building, and probably four or five versions of each of those strategies on the site, before determining the proper design direction. As the design evolves, multiple studies are undertaken at each step along the way, such that the process would resemble a branching tree if you were to diagram it. These days, when architects talk about process it's often in a determinist sense or the result of some algorithm—"I plug in this variable and that variable, and the building comes out." But even in the most extreme examples of this approach, there is obviously an intuitive overlay, a point at which someone is saying, "Okay, let's move this here, and do this differently there," making intuitive judgments and so on, and that's really the part that I find more interesting. How do things come to look or be the way they are? I am always fascinated by this question, especially in the natural world. I collect books on evolutionary theory and development, and to a large extent my design process is patterned on something like random variation and natural selection, in which the process is directed by intuition and project-specific forces. I am not using process to legitimize the results, nor to make claims for the architecture. There is a tendency for architects—particularly young architects—to exaggerate the amount of invention in their work, because I think there is pressure to be viewed as avant-garde to get noticed. I don't share this concern.

RM: I'm struck by the decision to include your rough design sketches in the book. One wonders why more architects don't publish their own drawings. The suggestion seems to be that preliminary design is now done on-screen. The virtual manipulation of three-dimensional volumes has replaced the old-school model that began with the diagram or sketch. It's clear from the built projects (and their renderings) that you are anything but technophobic. So what point are you making with the sketches?

JR: I think the sketches are important in that they capture something essential about the project in a very concise way, just as other aspects are better shown in a model or diagram. Also, without exception it is how I start every project, and I think it is important to show the beginning if you are talking about the work. As I said before, I will go through hundreds and hundreds of sketches in the course of a project, particularly at the beginning, so if one is pulled out for presentation, it is not to imply that it is precious in some Beaux Arts kind of way, but that it is representative of a certain stage of the process and is valuable to the extent that it illustrates that moment. It's an interesting question, because it implies that you don't really need to draw by hand anymore, which sounds strange to me. I like to draw; for me it's a mode of thinking. In the office we try to use as many tools as possible during the course of the design process—physical models, digital models, and diagrams—without being too dependent on any one tool or technique. Sometimes it's not clear when the architect is in control of the tool and when the tool is in control of the architect—it's best to avoid this situation. The great value I see in computers is that they allow you to explore so many more possibilities in a shorter period of time. I think every architect practicing today started with hand tools and has transitioned, to some degree or another, to digital tools. The next generation of architects will likely produce someone who has never drawn by hand, only with digital tools, at which point it will get very interesting.

RM: You've built a school on the South Side of Chicago and proposed one for New Jersey, and the Chicago Public Schools system has commissioned you to develop a new prototype high school. Do you structure your responses to program in relation to a specific educational philosophy?

JR: I am very interested in the ideas of Howard Gardner, who came up with the theory of multiple intelligences, which basically says that there are different kinds of intelligence—mathematical, spatial, linguistic, and so on—and that people learn in different ways. The Gary Comer Youth Center is an example of an application of these ideas in architectural terms, with spaces for developing different kinds of intelligence—physical, mathematical, musical, kinesthetic—all pressed up against one another cheek by jowl. The building provides multiple platforms for different types of learning without segregating the kids who use them or applying a hierarchy to those platforms. I would be very interested in building a school predicated on Gardner's theories, but they are somewhat controversial within the education world, where there's no shortage of competing philosophies. More often than not, school design is reflective of the attitudes of those running the school, with teacher-student interaction being a key attribute. Charter and private schools by and large seek to maximize student-teacher interaction and tend to be more open-minded about how the design reflects their educational philosophies. Public schools by comparison tend to be rigid in their thinking and in their application of guidelines and standards, which often stifle creativity and discourage change. In their defense, they are operating in an environment in which security is a primary issue as a precondition to learning, and the building design often reflects this reality.

RM: You once described a favorite moment at the Gary Comer Youth Center—looking down from the second floor Rec Room, through the cafeteria windows into the double-height volume where would-be Jordans shoot around in the midst of the Drill Team members twirling flags and wooden rifles. Cross-programming at its best. Yet the projects are almost always drawn and photographed from the outside—as objects in a field. Is there a tension between your complex interior admixtures and their far simpler exteriors?

JR: Yes, I guess this is an example of what I mean by formal simplicity yielding spatial complexity, but the question really gets back to the media and how projects are represented. The internal spatial experience that you are describing—being in one space and looking into a second space through a third space—is the key spatial attribute of the project but a quality that is very difficult to photograph. On the other hand, the building exterior is easily photographed and easy to talk about, so invariably this is the image that everyone sees and what one reads about, but it is only part of the story and maybe not the most interesting part. The thing about the youth center was that the building's users didn't want any windows (too many drive-by shootings in the neighborhood), so the challenge was how to bring daylight into the interior in interesting ways so that it felt light and airy despite having few windows and consequently how to animate large windowless expanses of wall on the outside. To some extent the building is divided into exterior and interior experiences, but unavoidably so, given the circumstances. The Poetry Foundation is an example of a project in which these experiences are not easily separated, but it too will probably be difficult to photograph.

RM: In your Old Post Office proposal, there is a reference to a painting, *Isle of the Dead* by Arnold Böcklin. It is the only extra-architectural reference that I've run across with respect to your work. Would you agree that your references are culled from the discipline of architecture itself, versus from biology, philosophy, topography, et cetera? Why?

JR: In general, I'm not interested in reading buildings by metaphor or analogy; my work does not generally draw on outside elements for inspiration. That being said, sometimes I will make references to communicate the ideas of the project, once they are in place. For example, the Böcklin montage in the Old Post Office, to communicate the idea of the connection of place and ritual, or the metaphor of a driftwood stick for the House on the Lake, or the analogy of an organism for the Perth Amboy High School, where the towers are the vital organs and the classroom bars are the tissue. These metaphors explain the architecture but do not necessarily generate it.

    I am most interested in the physical aspects of the work—the experience of space and the materiality that engenders it. I have no interest in trying to make a building that is a three-dimensional representation of some abstract theory; nor am I interested in making a building that looks like an animal or is anthropomorphic in some way. I think it's ironic that people describe this kind of work as organic, because nothing could be further from the truth—a fish looks like a fish because it's a fish. Similarly, if a building is to be read, then I think that reading should grow out of the way it is made and directly experienced.

RM: Teaching offers many architects respite from the frantic pace of the real world. Some think of it as a laboratory where ideas are tested; others consider it a place where students learn techniques (real or virtual), and now there's considerable talk about the so-called research studio. I'm guessing that your studios fall somewhere in the middle: grounded in the real, yet not technocentric; insistent on ideas, yet leery of endless research. How do you run your IIT studios?

JR: This is a very interesting question and something I struggle with every year—what is the purpose of a design studio? Is it a laboratory, as you say, for uncovering new ideas? Is it a course where you teach someone how to be a designer or whatever that means? I think the answer to this question changes depending on prevailing conditions within the profession. When I was a student, the profession looked to the academies for inspiration and the way forward. This is clearly not the case today. Due to technological advances, new materials, processes, and techniques, and global capital, the real world is conceiving and realizing projects that were previously unimaginable. The profession is not looking to the academy today, but just the opposite; the academy is imitating what they see going on in the profession. This calls into question the laboratory model, which too often is used as a way for faculty to flatter themselves. I am suspicious of the so-called research studio that rarely makes it beyond research to analysis and then to application, and when it does, it looks suspiciously like what Rem Koolhaas was doing in 1989. To me this is not much different than teaching what Mies was doing in 1960. On the other hand, I do not think you can teach a person to be a designer, but you can teach methodology, so I suppose that is what I do. I try to get the students to focus on space rather than form. The studios are always set up to foreground some particular aspect of design, such as the relationship of the building to landscape, for example, and students will research a broad set of forces that impact that design—programmatic, site, social, political, environmental, and so on—and determine what is important for them. My studios without exception have a material investigation component in which students research a material or constructional system, explore its potential, and then apply that research to the project. Also, there is typically some social component either embedded into the program or more overtly stated—like a cemetery for the unclaimed, for instance—that they have to consider. The point is that architecture can reside in any or all of these areas, and by setting the table in this way it allows students to find their own voice and prompts them to ask themselves what their work is about.

A Chicago Architect
Brad Lynch

In September 2006, Ronan asked me and my family to attend a performance of
A Prairie Home Companion at the recently completed Gary Comer Youth Center. He did so
without knowing that we were fans of the show and that there was a personal connection
for me. Twenty-five years earlier, I was renovating a nineteenth-century farmhouse in
Highland, Wisconsin, which is situated between Dodgeville and Spring Green. Dodgeville is
the corporate home of Lands' End, the company that Gary Comer founded and a long-time
sponsor of *A Prairie Home Companion*; and Spring Green is where Taliesin, Frank Lloyd
Wright's home and school, is located. The farmhouse interior was a construction site, and
it is where I both worked and lived by myself for almost a year. My closest neighbor was
almost a mile away, and other than books, my only companion was the radio and a record
player. Saturday nights I would make bread, drink a good part of a case of Huber beer,
and listen to the show on the radio. I believed, with my simple surroundings, geographic
isolation, and the arctic wind blowing across the farm fields, that this radio show was
written for my own personal enjoyment. A couple decades later, I found that even the kids
were amused by it.

The previous summer, John had given me a personal tour of the center as it was
nearing completion, and I was duly impressed if not a bit envious. The building incorporated
everything you would expect from a well-funded institutional project and much more.
Detailed by a skillful and thoughtful hand, it was a resolved work of architecture in every
way, and it had integrated a complex program that continued to develop as the project
was being designed. As we toured the building, I listened to John talk about the various
functions of the space, their architectural relationships, and the things that had stemmed
from the client's goals. You could tell that this was more than a commission for him; it
was a personal endeavor, and I couldn't help but smile as he told me for whom the building
was designed and how it would be used.

This building could have been built anywhere in the city, or in any other city for
that matter, and still have been a meaningful piece of architecture. It still would have won
awards and recognition and been cited for its quiet integration of sustainable technology,
spatial composition, and careful detailing of materials. But this building was not built
anywhere else; it was built in the worst neighborhood of the South Side of Chicago.
Before Gary Comer returned to his childhood neighborhood to bestow it with this center
along with a hundred new and renovated homes and a future charter high school (also by
Ronan), the safest havens were the adjacent Chicago Skyway, an interstate highway that
hovers thirty feet above street level, or the locked freight cars that move slowly underneath
it. The day I visited with John, the construction crews were working on the final finishes
and installations. There weren't many end users around, but there were enough that you
did get a strong sense of this building being an oasis in a desert of hard living and constant
tragedy, and of its potential to change lives if not save them.

It seemed an ominous drive west on Seventy-Second Avenue with my family on
the night of the performance, in a neighborhood I had never been in after dark. As we
approached the Gary Comer Youth Center, the potential for what this building could be

for the neighborhood was no longer a concept but a striking reality. The center's name scrolled in LED lights on top of a tower that had become a beacon in the community both figuratively and literally. The colored cement panels that clad the massive, unbroken exterior volumes held vibrancy; when lit at night, they are reminiscent of the colors of the flags used by the South Shore Drill Team, for whom the center was built. There is a playful mixture of transparency and color as light pours through horizontal glass slits that punctuate the cement panels. That glass (and all of the other glass with street exposure) is bulletproof, and the concrete panels are easily replaceable if they are vandalized. In the end, there was probably no need for these measures, as the building has not suffered ill will or abuse—only respect. This respect was evident in everyone, from the neighborhood volunteers who guided people where to park their cars in the vacant lot across the street to the volunteer ushers whose gesticulations, movements, and steps were perhaps a little livelier and their backs slightly straighter with pride. When Garrison Keillor began the show in honor of Gary Comer, it was an intermingled crowd of affluent northsiders, people involved with the project, families of the Drill Team, residents of the neighborhood, the center's staff, and, of course, the Drill Team members. Comer was too ill to attend the event, but he was able to view it by video feed from his bed. Studs Terkel was a guest, and among the many performers there was the Gary Comer Youth Center Voices, who sang "Oh Happy Day," and, of course, the South Shore Drill Team performed, which must have been mysterious for the radio audience but powerful for those in attendance. Whether the whole audience was accustomed to Keillor's dry humor or biting commentary was irrelevant. For those involved with the center, it was an evening of hope, realized and recognized. There was more at work here than the architecture, but it was the architecture that gave life and a home to the philanthropic ideals of the client. No one there had to understand what the motivation or theory was behind the architecture. It was self-evident, and it was powerful.

The program for the Comer Center had grown from being a simple gym for the Drill Team into a multifunctional space for supporting community and educational services. How was John able to win such a commission and able to work with such a generous patron? He had won the well-publicized competition for the Perth Amboy, New Jersey High School the year before, beating out the likes of Thom Mayne and Peter Eisenman, neither of whom had ever heard of this young Chicagoan. Many ideas represented in that school design are recognizable in the built Comer Center, but the Perth Amboy school remains to be realized. Perhaps the root of why John was so successful with the Comer Center—and was able to gain the trust of a client/patron that we would all clamor to have—is his ability to comfortably convey the essence of his process and clarify the design concept to share the ideals of the client.

When John received the opportunity to submit his credentials to design the Akiba-Schechter Jewish Day School in the Hyde Park neighborhood of Chicago in 2002, he seemed an unlikely choice. He had only a few projects under his belt, no school experience, let alone a completed stand-alone building, and the architects he was competing against primarily did school buildings. He was able to convince the board, which included an architect, to visit two of his projects with him. For John, these spaces conveyed a developing and recurring theme of adaptability and flexibility across multiple functions that, when activated by a specific use, did not deter from the holistic architectural aesthetic or design intent. The first project they visited was the Catholic Extension Chapel in Chicago, only 750 square feet in size; it illustrates John's approach to creating programmatically flexible space in a chapel for a Catholic missionary organization occupying office space downtown. This straightforward design features a wall of operable maple panels that hide support spaces, while religious services take place but pivot open to reveal equipment and a kitchen when the space is being used for other functions.

The second space John visited with the school board was a renovation of a masonry coach house that was to be transformed into a new space that needed to perform an array of functions for a growing young family that lived in the house at the front of the same lot. Here, he clearly demonstrates his ability to design open, well-lit spaces, with simple volumetric insertions that seem to come from the mind of a skilled cabinetmaker. These insertions were millwork cabinets of light birch that handled the equipment and storage needs; as they open and close, move and slide, they activate the particular function that may be required. Standing in the interior of the coach house, John was able to explain how a beautifully simple space could be realized, with a very similar approach to spatial organization for the multifunctional needs of the school. They believed him.

Building Form

John began his working career in Chicago in 1985 at the offices of Tigerman Fugman McCurry Architects (later renamed Tigerman McCurry), after completing undergraduate school at the University of Michigan. He sat directly across from Stanley Tigerman. He easily survived the authoritative commentary and critical scrutiny and thus became enlisted in a venerable consortium of Chicago architects who had worked for Tigerman early in their careers, including James Nagle, Laurence Booth, Ralph Johnson, and David Woodhouse. For the most part, their work has not been influenced by the historicism and irony that makes up much of Tigerman's oeuvre, nor did they follow his powerful voice in architectural theory and education. In fact, they all have taken a different individualistic approach to architecture, and with perhaps the exception of Booth, all unapologetically modern; however, it does say a great deal about Tigerman's capability as a mentor, a talent that his former protégés, including John, willingly acknowledge.

After almost two years at Tigerman Fugman McCurry, John left Chicago—a city he originally chose to work in because of its size and proximity to his hometown of Grand Rapids, Michigan—to study at Harvard's Graduate School of Design, where he received his Master's of Architecture in 1991. After the Harvard experience, John decided to return to Chicago, but this time not out of geographical convenience. In his three years of graduate school, he had an opportunity to critically compare Chicago to other cities and made a conscious decision to make it his home, with an end desire to start his own firm there. He landed a job at Krueck + Sexton Architects, a firm that had only recently been in the national architectural conscious and whose founding principal, Ron Krueck, steadfastly held onto an idiom of modernism as a basis for design investigation in the 1980s, when most other firms in Chicago lost their bearing and explored a Chinese takeout menu of postmodernism. In that era, Krueck was admired and became a beacon of hope for a few young Chicagoans who didn't believe in the postmodern approach, myself being one of them. So it is presumably here that John grew his molars in setting a design direction for himself and further developed the impetus to begin his own firm, but before doing so, he needed an opportunity to hone his project management skills on large projects. This he accomplished at Lohan Associates, where the firm's namesake is none other than the grandson of Ludwig Mies van der Rohe. After three years with Lohan, he established his own firm in 1999, beginning with an apartment renovation in a historic building on East Lake Shore Drive.

Curiously for someone who believes that the current laboratory of ideas is the real world, John makes a concerted effort to regularly teach graduate seminars and studios at the Illinois Institute of Technology (IIT), where he is a tenured professor. He preaches what he practices in that he encourages visionary concepts for real world projects, but the work is anchored in the pragmatic resolve of building technology and craftsmanship in the use of materials. He is not mired in architectural rhetoric, either in his firm or with his students, and it is perhaps why I have witnessed more clarity from his students than in most reviews of recent years.

He met his wife Clare Lyster, also an architect, during student reviews at IIT in 2002. Clare's work leans toward a more academic approach to site, urbanism, and landscape; she is a professor at the University of Illinois at Chicago. It is a pleasure to be around them, as they seem to keep a balance between practice and academia. They have a gentle understanding of what each other does and do not compete for attention. It must be said that a couple that can go fly-fishing together can probably get through the idiosyncrasies of being in the same profession and living under the same roof—and love what they do.

Crafting Space

Given John's background and quiet wisdom it is not difficult to understand how he could obtain the Akiba-Schechter commission and make a great success of it as his first new construction project. He delivered on the expectations that he originally established with the school board, to deliver adaptability along with a sense of identity and place. Although limited in budget, it was an opportunity for John to advance his exploration of materials, spatial layering, and complexity without the limitations placed by the form of an existing building envelope. It gives an indication of the foundations of his upcoming projects. When given an existing building to repurpose, such as the behemoth Old Chicago Post Office that remains vacant after a decade, John came up with perhaps one of the most clever ideas for Visionary Chicago Architecture in 2003[1]: to convert 2.5 million square feet of concrete, limestone, and steel into an urban burial site made up of chapels, crypts, and a voluminous remembrance hall. With its base and underbelly clad in monumental sheets of COR-TEN steel, highway commuters would drive through a vast opening of the building as funeral processions arrive by river barge and enter the building through a sequence of ramps and monumental gates of steel to cathedral-like proportions of the re-created post-office lobby. The deft handling of the juxtaposition of new and old materials, the articulation of new space against old, and the balance between human scale and monumentality bring to mind the work of Carlo Scarpa in Venice. Under closer examination, this is John's individual approach of working in appropriate materials to define the spatial composition at a large scale while maintaining control of the design as the details become more minute and hold together the original design concept.

Rising above the Old Post Office and along its existing expanse, the design shows a cladding of metal webbing that transforms the facade into a gateway to downtown from the western suburbs. One cannot help but reference the gates of Paris, but it is quintessentially Chicago in its ingenuity, monumentality, and sheer size. Although the project will most likely not be realized, the design of this gateway represents some of the soundest ideas to be found in contemporary Chicago architecture, and it signals a much-needed change of the architectural guard in Chicago, with Ronan clearly at the forefront of this group.
In the best sense, he is part of a new generation of architects steeped in Chicago tradition in that he is curious, grounded, pragmatic, rigorous, and self-critical but also innovative and inventive. Certainly these are the qualities of talented architects working in an array of other cities, but there is a long history in Chicago of celebrating architecture as a building art, not merely a graphic one, and where rhetoric and argot are ultimately supplanted by a steady course of construction and a concern for getting things done. John has established himself as a noteworthy architect not by being influenced by stylistic perceptions or fussy permutations of forms but by having a deliberate, slow consistency throughout his projects. They are embedded with craftsmanship, materiality, and a gift for spatial composition and clarity. The advantage of his work is that it is of the time, yet it will age with grace and dignity and continue to have relevance long after the awards and press clippings are filed.

As of this writing there are a succession of private homes that John has designed along with three high schools and a building to celebrate poetry, all of which are about to begin construction. All are instilled with a quiet elegance and skill that come from a Chicago architect with a steady hand and a measured ego. These buildings will be meaningful additions to their environs and hold significant value to the clients and end users. They will be slightly better than his last group of buildings and no less important. The next set of buildings will not only be relevant, they will be necessary.

1   Stanley Tigerman and William Martin asked fourteen architects to design seven gateways to the city on behalf of the Chicago Central Area Committee; they published the results in a book called *Visionary Chicago Architecture: Fourteen Inspired Concepts for the Third Millennia* in December 2004. The architects were separated into two groups of seven. One group was considered older and more established, and the other was younger and less established. Each member of one group had a different gateway project assigned to them, and those projects were paralleled in the other group. John Ronan, as part of the younger group, was assigned the Old Post Office.

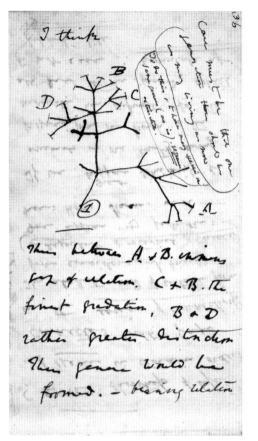

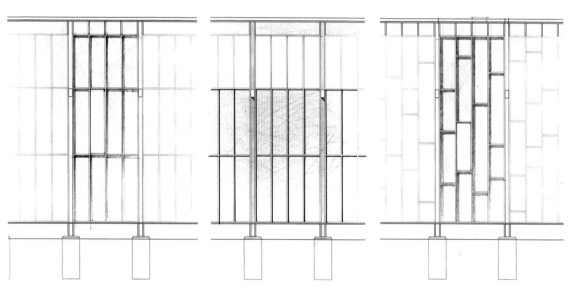

Framing option A

Framing option B

Framing option C

Contingency

Why is an elephant like an elephant and not like a horse? The first diagram on the opposite page is by Charles Darwin; it describes the process by which evolution works. [01] Darwin studied how pigeon breeders produced particular attributes in their birds and suspected that nature might work in a similar way. Read from bottom to top, the line moves through a series of branching pathways to divergent endpoints; read from top to bottom, any one of the outlying points can be traced back to its origin in a linear fashion.

    This is also true of design. Each stage in the design process is dependent upon all of the steps that preceded it, and while it would be difficult to predict the many possible outcomes at the outset, it is rather easy to trace the development of the end result backwards to the beginning of the process in a seemingly linear way. This selectively edited version is typically the way a design story is told; the dead ends and broken branches of the process are edited out in favor of the streamlined version that moves inexorably to its logical conclusion.

    In actuality design develops along the same contingent pathways found in the natural world. The drawing studies in the bottom figure on the opposite page represent three of a number of possible wall configurations. [02A–C] They were generated more or less randomly in response to the question: how should the wall be framed? The study on the far right was ultimately selected as the one best adapted to the project conditions for a number of reasons. It will be built by unskilled labor and requires less precision. It allows greater flexibility in the placement of windows. The bridging between framing members is easier to install; the wall allows placement of objects within it by people of varying heights; it offers individuality to each bay and so on. In this way, project conditions acting as causal agents impart direction to an otherwise random process. This direction, in turn, triggers other studies whose resolution is embedded in the object and becomes part of a history that cannot be erased.

This book will attempt to show some of that history, acknowledging the conditional aspects of the design process that occur within each project. At another level, it will attempt to show how each project is contingent in some way on the projects that preceded it. Working forward from earlier projects to more recent ones, it illustrates how tendencies emerge and themes develop through time and over the course of many projects.

The answer to the horse versus elephant question, according to Darwin, is that through an iterative process over many generations, circumstances have shaped organisms to be uniquely adapted to their environment. Darwin proposed the mechanisms of random variation and natural selection to explain how organisms evolve over time and to account for the resulting diversity of the natural world. Random variation is a nondirectional tendency of genetic mutation that creates the minor differences that are the raw material for evolutionary change. Natural selection then provides the cause. Organisms with more favorable traits live to reproduce, and these traits thereby become more common in successive generations. The results vary, but the process remains the same.

Each of the projects included in this book is a response to a unique set of issues and circumstances, but they are all the result of a design process that is more or less the same from project to project. Themes evolve over the course of multiple projects, with each one in some way conditional on the work that preceded it. [03]

[03]

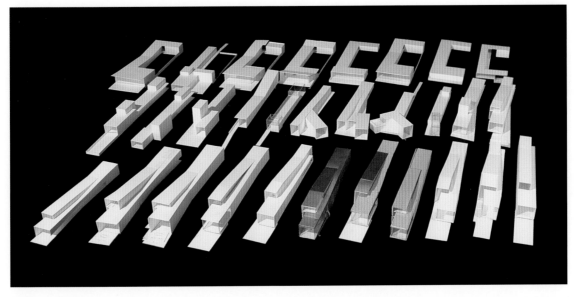

Coach House

(1999–2000)

Lincoln Park neighborhood, Chicago, Illinois

This project, the renovation of a one-hundred-year-old coach house, explores programmatic adaptation. The existing structure—untouched since it last housed horses and coachmen—stands on an alley behind the main building in the Lincoln Park neighborhood of Chicago. The owners, a couple with three small children, had numerous plans for the space: a playroom, office, media room, conference room, party space, and guest bedroom. The limited square footage would not allow for the separate inclusion of all of these programs, but carving the structure into small rooms would have destroyed the original spatial qualities.

A strategy of indeterminacy was established whereby the space was kept open and flexible so that the program could alternate between playroom, guesthouse, media room, or conference space as the family's needs dictated. Support requirements for these various programs were subsumed into a series of furniture-like elements that were then inserted into the space. These millwork pieces provide storage areas for toys, media equipment, and coats at the front of the house; kitchen appliances are concealed in the center portion; the rear of the space converts to a guest suite with a foldout bed, closet, and writing desk.

The project maintains a distinction between the more persistent masonry shell and the ephemeral interior construction that may change many times over the life of the space.

Preexisting structure

Birch was chosen for the flooring and millwork due to its tendency to darken from light pink to a rich amber over time, against the more stable coloration of the masonry. Materials will age; use will leave its residue; and other changes will also take place, both relentless and imperceptible to the human eye. The interior construction will endure, until it gives way to some new reality when the cycle will begin again.

New skylights highlight the existing
masonry with raking light.

Concept sketch

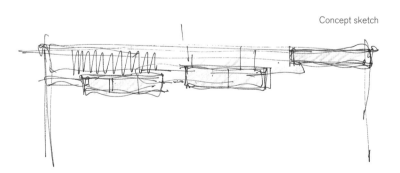

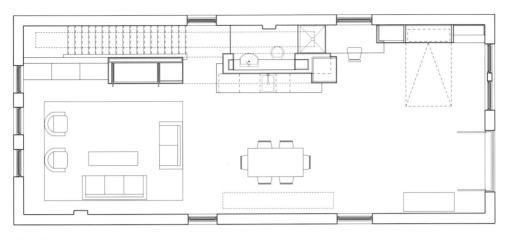

Second-floor plan

0 2' 4'   8'

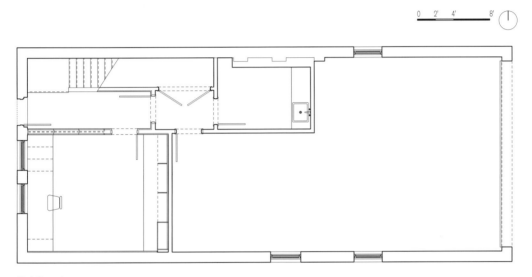

First-floor plan

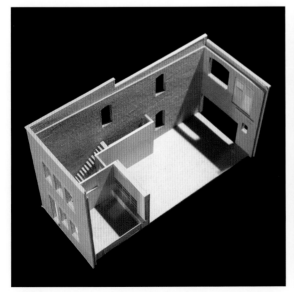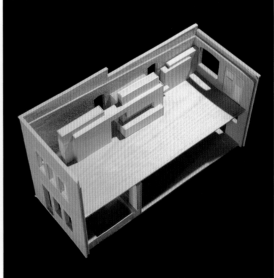

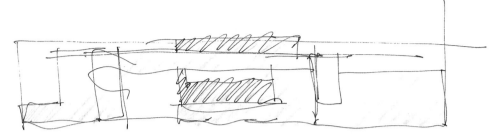

Elevation sketch

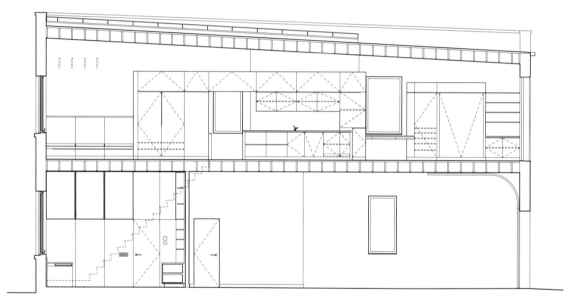

Building section

opposite: A glass ceiling in the
bathroom at the top of the stairs
admits natural light from the new
skylights, which are cut into the roof
to expose the original framing.

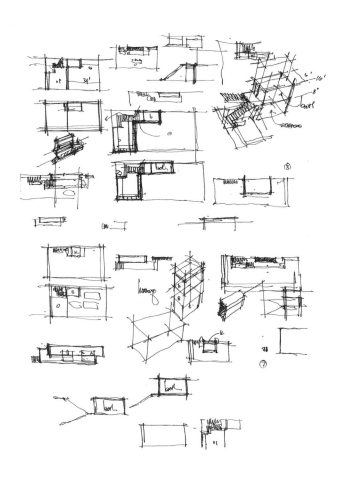

Second floor in section and plan

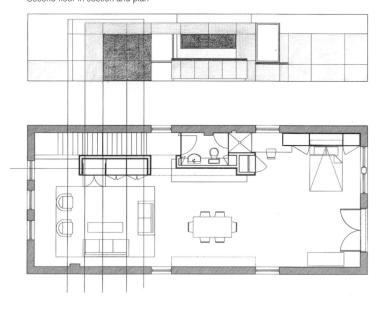

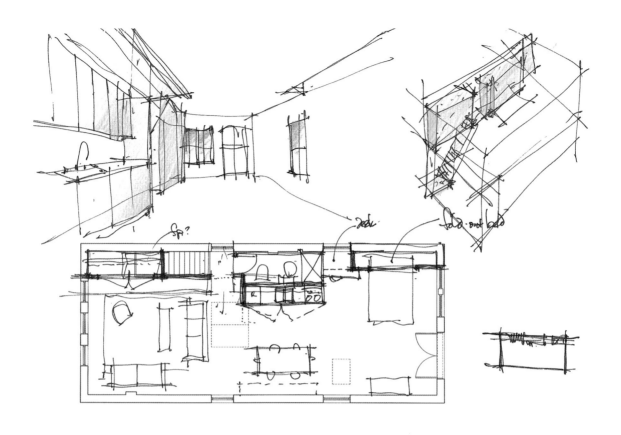

Deployable guest area with foldout
bed, closet, and desk

Millwork insertions to conceal
support functions

Built-in second-floor media storage
and kitchen

House on the Edge of a Forest

(2000–2001)

Northbrook, Illinois

Situated on the edge of a forest preserve, this house explores the relationship between site, material, and program. The property is urban on one side but falls away toward a forest preserve on the other, yielding a building with two distinct characters: a low, private facade in front and an all-glass, two-story wall in the rear. Careful placement of the windows on the sides of the house maintains the illusion of solitude.

Bearing walls made from concrete block whose surface is ground to expose its limestone aggregate provide order within the house. These walls create a formal entry court on the exterior and serve as organizing devices on the interior, dividing the space into separate zones for service, living, and sleeping. The bearing walls also provide display space for the owner's art collection. The neutral surfaces of the house change character throughout the year, depending on the color of light reflecting off the trees: green in summer, orange and yellow in fall, and white in winter.

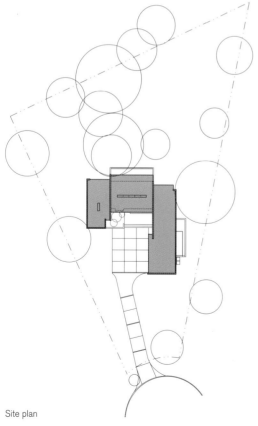

Site plan

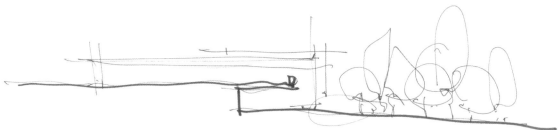

Early sketch

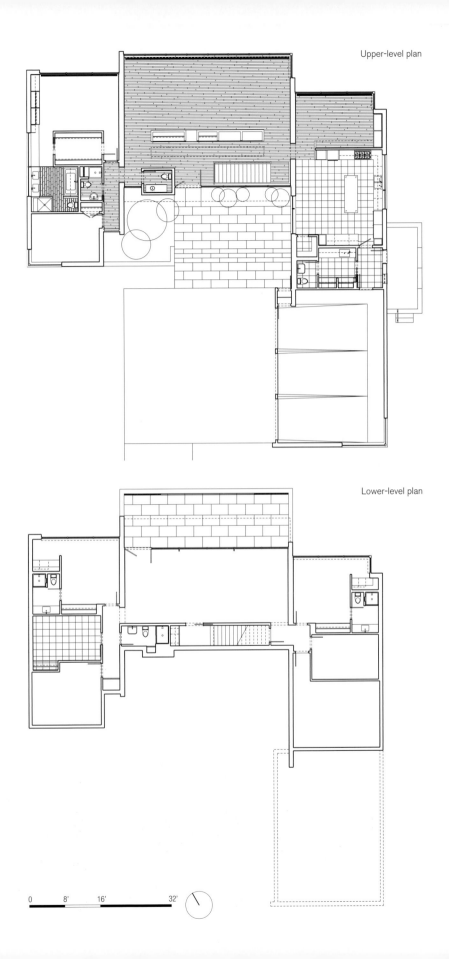

Upper-level plan

Lower-level plan

0   8'   16'   32'

Sketch of house/landscape
interface

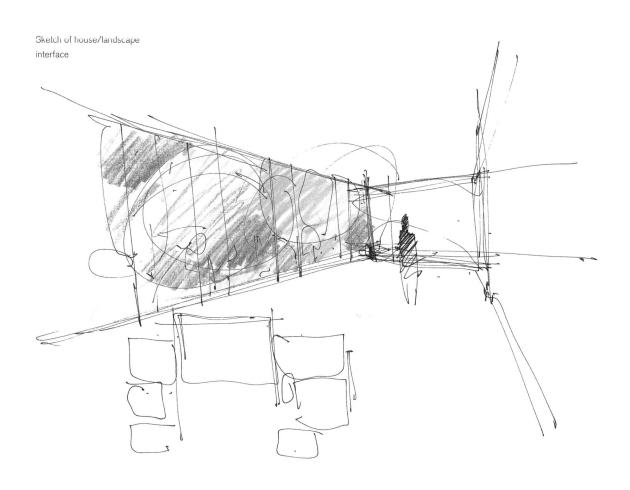

Views of the forest become a
painting by implication, whose colors
shift with the changing seasons.
Living spaces cantilever out into
the trees to increase the sense of
proximity to nature.

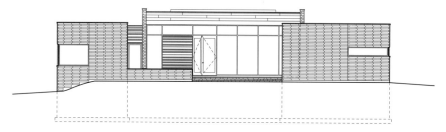

Street elevation

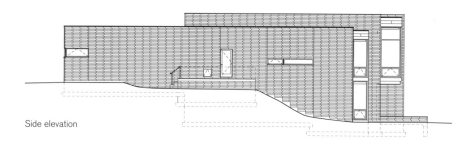

Side elevation

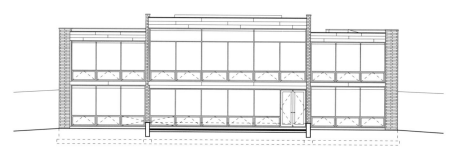

Forest elevation

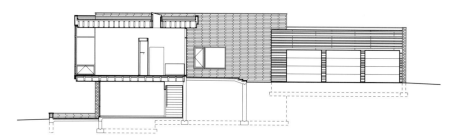

Section through courtyard

Akiba-Schechter Jewish Day School

(2000–2005)

Hyde Park neighborhood, Chicago, Illinois

This elementary school was one of our first nonresidential built projects. The school was looking for an enduring presence within its Hyde Park neighborhood and came to us with a wish list of spaces that was difficult to accommodate given the compressed urban site. We adopted a strategy of creating a programmatically adaptable space that could become an indoor playground, lunchroom, or assembly room with a deployable stage.

Built in two phases, the new elementary school was carefully sited to form a secure entry courtyard with the existing preschool and to create distinct programmatic zones for playing, congregating, and student drop-off.

In lieu of conventional construction, we adopted a form of construction typically relegated to industrial uses: structural precast concrete wall panels. Concrete form-retarders and power washing were used to expose the limestone aggregate and to create a dialogue with the solid limestone walls of the adjacent preschool. Laser-cut Hebrew letters cast into the concrete formwork communicate identity and give the school the sense of being permanently rooted in the community. The school came to view these panels as stone tablets. On the courtyard side of the building, preformed oxidized copper cladding was used to line the spaces where students, staff, and visitors come in direct contact with the building.

Together with the existing preschool,
the building forms a secure entry
courtyard.

Early sketch

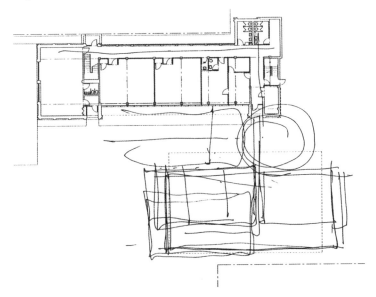

Oxidized copper panels clad the
north facade, while the remaining
three sides of the building are
structural precast concrete.

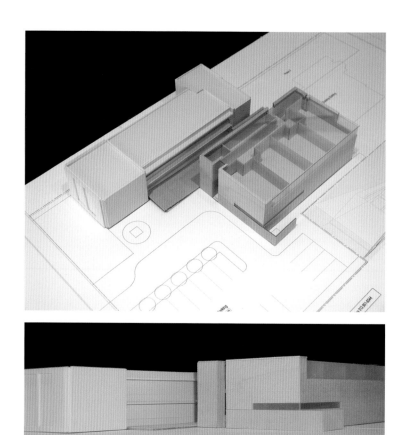

Early sketch of new and existing structures

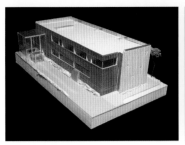
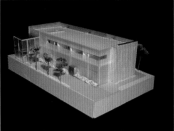

Materiality was explored in numerous models and mock-ups.

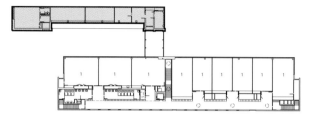

Second-floor plan

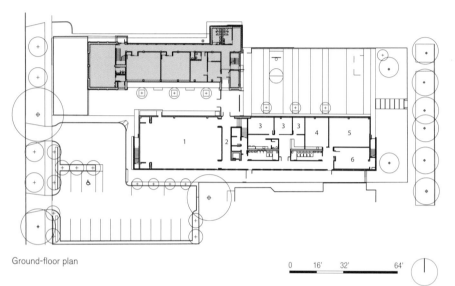

Ground-floor plan

1 Multipurpose room
2 Lobby
3 Offices
4 Science classroom
5 Library
6 Kitchen

0   16'   32'   64'

AKIBA

Some books leave us free and some books make us fr
- Ralph Waldo Emerson

A room without books
is like a body without a soul. - Cicero

In the good books, the point is not how many of them you can get through
rather how many can get through to you. - Mortimer Adler

Readers are plent thinkers are rare.
rriet Martineau

Precast panel erection

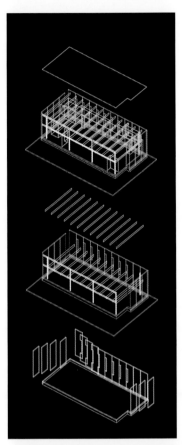

Exploded axonometric study of the
building structure

Concrete Townhouse

(2002–2004)

Lincoln Park neighborhood, Chicago, Illinois

This townhouse, built for a family of five, was an attempt to create a spacious, light-filled structure within a dense urban site. It also explores the gradation of space from communal to private. A formal entry zone on the first floor at the front of the house leads to a more casual family space overlooking a hardscape courtyard in the rear. Sliding glass panels between the family room and courtyard create a large indoor-outdoor living space, and a walnut staircase leads from this semipublic area to a children's playroom, from which the bedrooms are entered in a sequence from communal to private. The facade projects an image of openness and optimism and allows for views to the street.

Our approach to materiality was to explore the idea of imperfection. Pursuing a strategy of variegation, exterior walls are made of board-formed concrete in which pattern, texture, and even bug holes are valued over smooth perfection. As a result of constructing numerous mock-ups and material studies using cedar boards of varying textures and moisture content, a surface of light and dark was created to contrast with the clean precision of the building's aluminum and glass window framing.

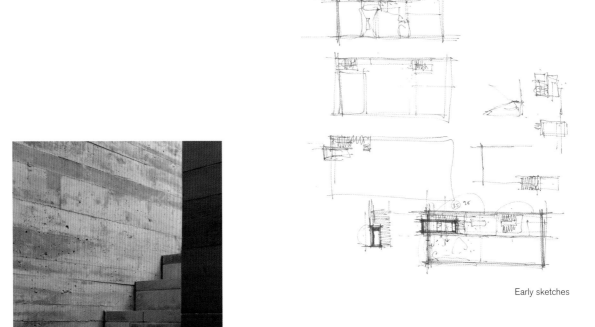

Early sketches

Glass wall panels open to an exterior
courtyard that is conceived as a
split-level outdoor living room, with
board-formed concrete walls, wood
screens, and a limestone fireplace.

Early sketches

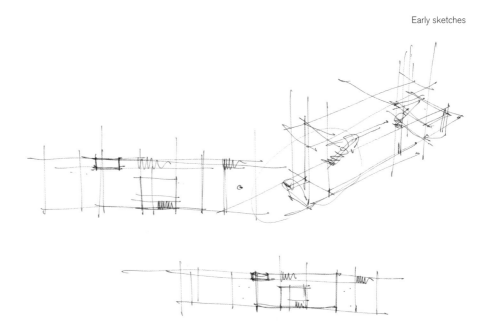

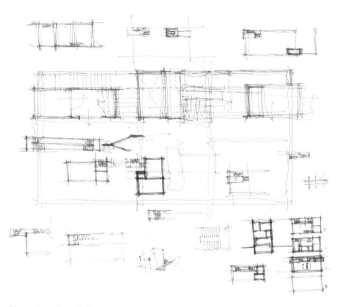

Plan and section studies

Third-floor plan

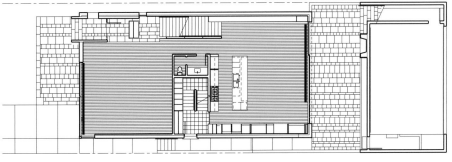

Second-floor plan

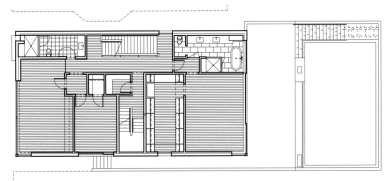

First-floor plan

0   5'   10'   20'

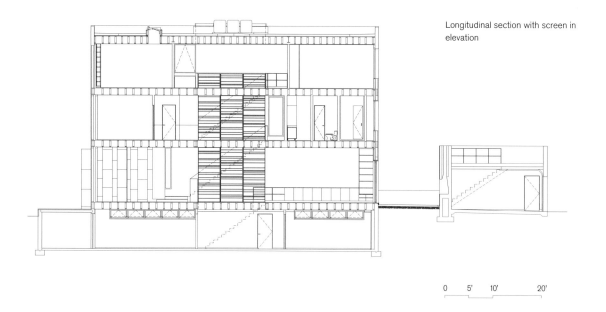

Longitudinal section with screen in elevation

0   5'   10'   20'

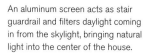

An aluminum screen acts as stair guardrail and filters daylight coming in from the skylight, bringing natural light into the center of the house.

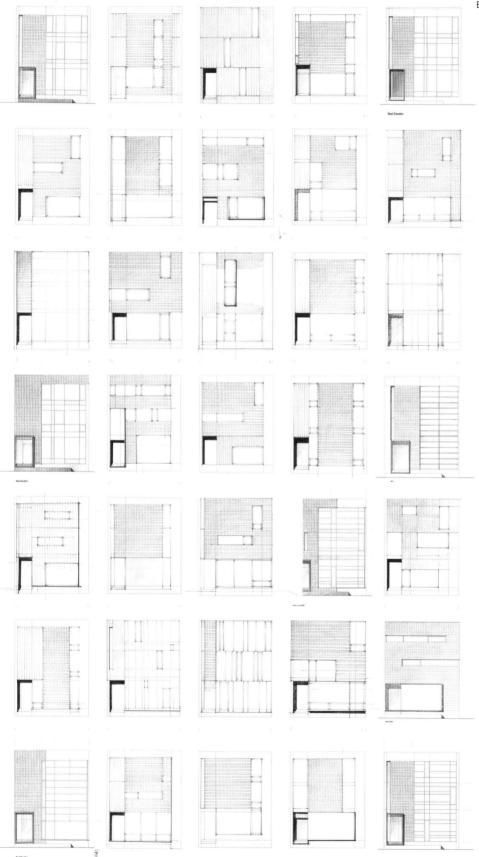

Early facade studies

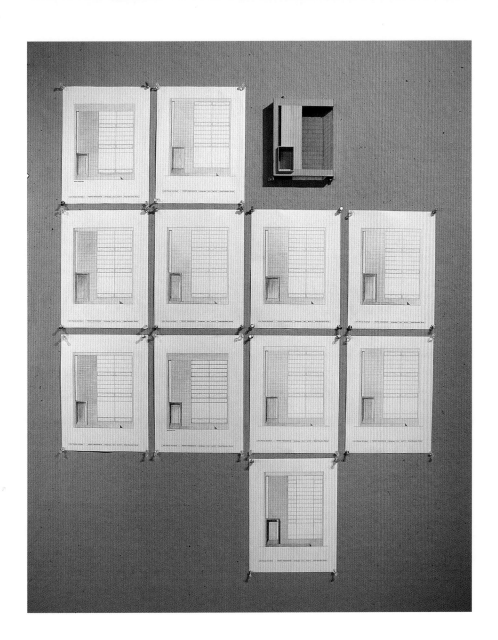

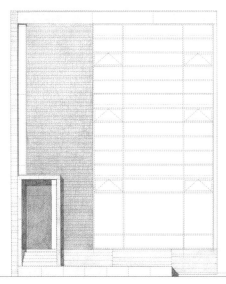

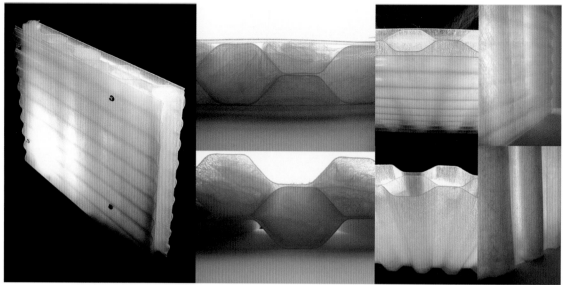

Materiality

While working on an elementary school and researching possible materials for the exterior cladding of a recreation space, we came across a composite plastic made of a polymer and glass-fiber reinforcing [01A–D]. The material is commonly used as wall cladding in commercial kitchens. It seemed appropriate for the recreation area not only because it was affordable and durable, but also because its translucency enabled us to daylight the space. Noticing its exceptional strength, we began to explore its structural properties. Perhaps by corrugating and layering multiple sheets and then filling the voids with glass-fiber insulation, we thought, we could create a self-supporting panel that would eliminate the need for metal supports, thereby creating a continuous luminous surface.

This episode highlights one of the underlying conditions of contemporary architecture: the emergence of new materials and the reordering of traditional relationships between structure, space, and materials. The historical trajectory of building culture describes a movement away from simple monolithic construction systems toward layered assemblies of increasing complexity, where each material or composite is assigned a position and role that leverage its unique attributes in service to the whole. [02A–B]

For example, a disposable paper coffee cup is composed of just a few materials: paper, wax, ink, and a little bit of glue. It is a simple object that can be said to possess a complex material relationship. The paper—coated with wax to form a waterproof composite—is of a specific thickness that enables it to hold a certain amount of liquid. Its base is designed to provide the requisite support and stability. Its upper edge is rolled to create a comfortable user interface but also to aid it structurally. Unroll it, and watch the system weaken. Its form allows for stacking for efficient transport and is scaled to the human hand. The cup's space, structure, and materiality can be said to be in an interdependent relationship: the composite paper surface that engenders the space also provides its structure. Change any variable and the others change as well.

The majority of our projects explore layered construction and the manipulation of those constituent interdependent layers. The chapel projects, like the paper coffee cup, illustrate the role that new materials play in creating new interdependent conditions between structure, space, and materiality. [03A–B]

[03A-B]

Precast Chapel

(2003)

Speculative

This project arose out of an interest in exploring the spatial possibilities of standard precast concrete elements, specifically tees and planks. It attempts to create a condition of material and structural interdependency in an economical and easy-to-assemble worship space.

The parking lot of a typical big-box retailer serves as the testing ground for this investigation: a prototypical interfaith space to promote dialogue and religious understanding in an increasingly heterogeneous suburban environment. Situated in a public location where people from all faiths intersect, the chapel explores the notion of contemporary sacred space and challenges its users to engage in cross-cultural dialogue.

Preliminary sketches

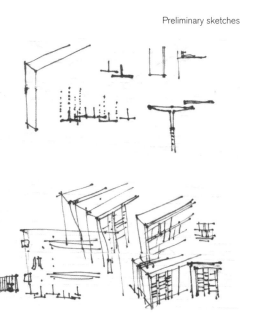

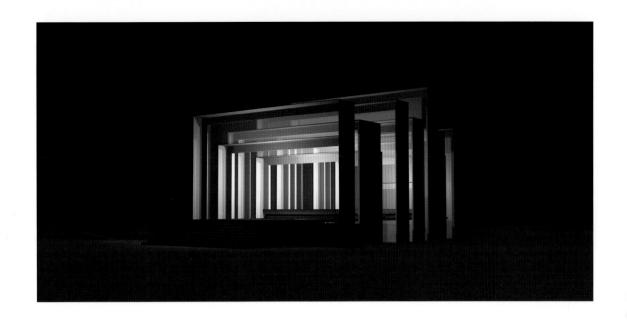

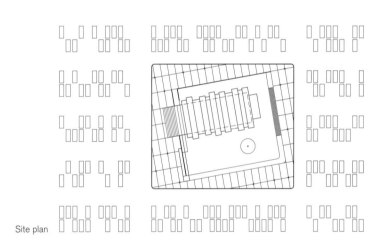

Site plan

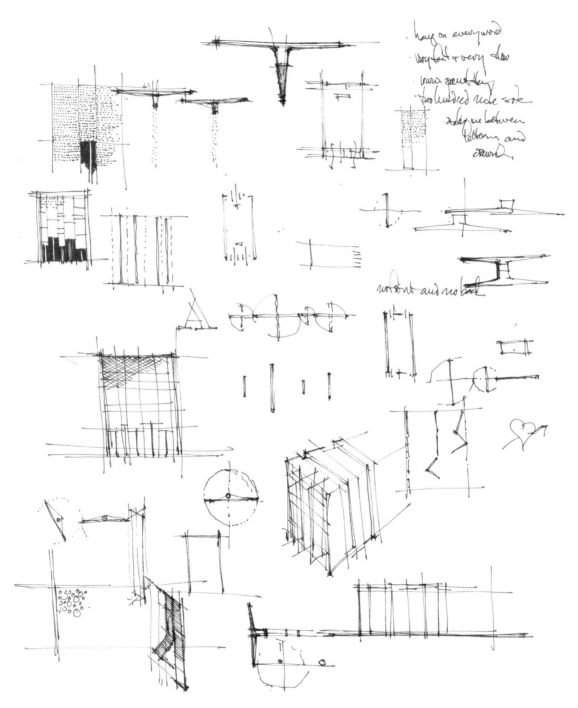

Early sketches

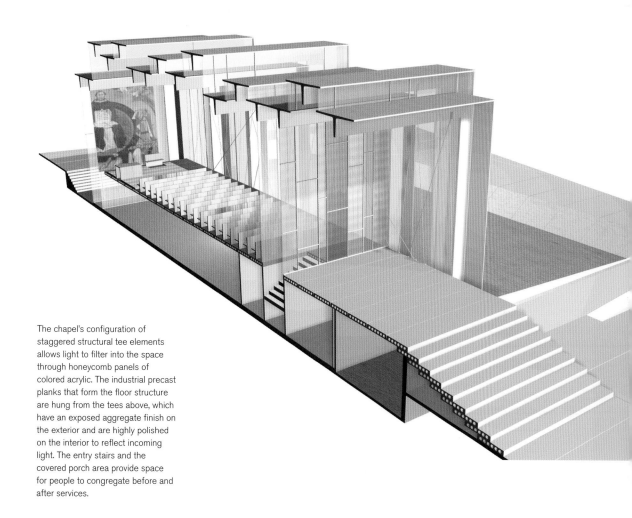

The chapel's configuration of staggered structural tee elements allows light to filter into the space through honeycomb panels of colored acrylic. The industrial precast planks that form the floor structure are hung from the tees above, which have an exposed aggregate finish on the exterior and are highly polished on the interior to reflect incoming light. The entry stairs and the covered porch area provide space for people to congregate before and after services.

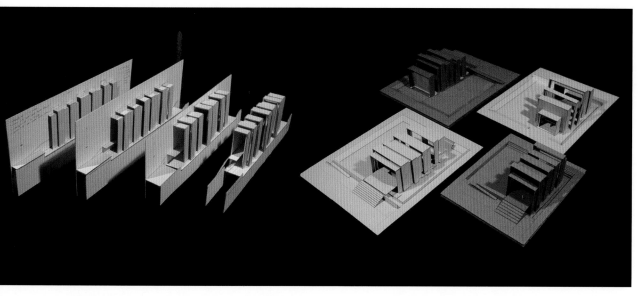

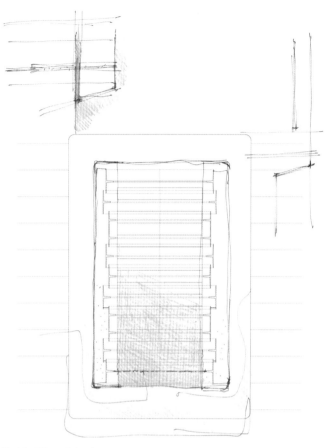

Sketch of the main level

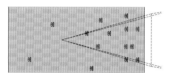

Islamic service

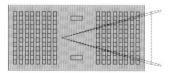

Neopagan service

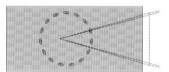

Buddhist service

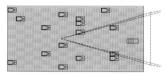

Christian service

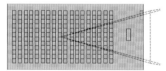

Jewish/Christian service

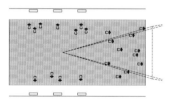

Hindu service

A deployable wooden floor allows for faith-specific seating configurations. With a modularity based on the size of a typical Islamic prayer rug, it can be manipulated into a variety of worship arrangements.

Hindu

Islamic

Buddhist

The back wall of the sanctuary acts
as a projection screen to customize
the space to each particular faith.

Christianity

Main-floor plan

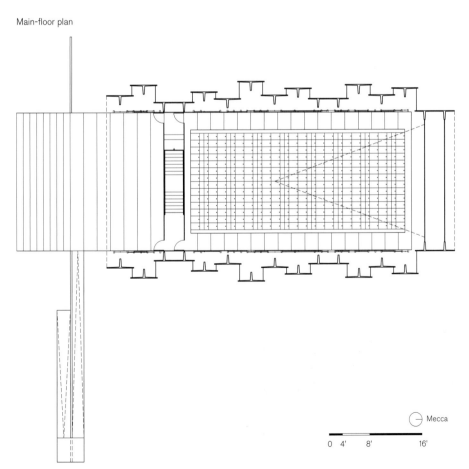

⊖ Mecca

0 4'   8'   16'

Drawing studies

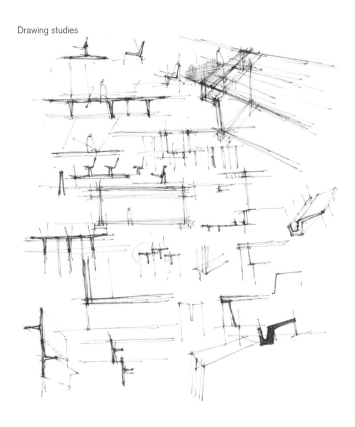

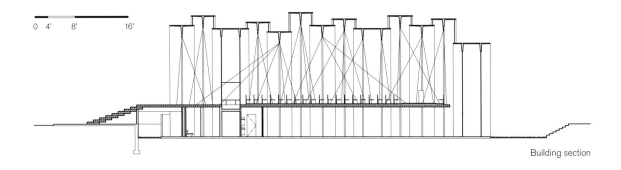

0 4' 8'   16'

Building section

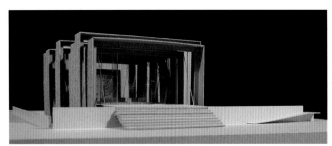

A sunken gravel courtyard around
the building provides outdoor space
for community gatherings.

THE MONASTIC DAY ACCORDING TO THE RULE OF SAINT BENEDICT

The Cistercian Ecclesiastica officia in the twelfth century. La documentation cistercienne, vol. 22, Reiningue, 1989.

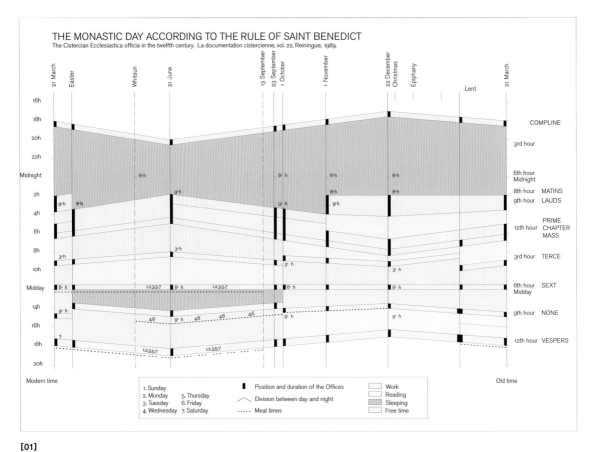

[01]

Adaptation

Several years ago, I came across a monastic timetable while doing research for a design studio I teach at IIT. Graphically it describes the relationship between time and space in a thirteenth-century Cistercian monastery. [01] The monastery is interesting from a programmatic standpoint in that each space supports a specific activity and bears a special name related to the program it supports—a refectory for eating, chapel for praying, chapter room for meeting, scriptorium for transcribing texts, and so on. The diagram describes when and for how long the monks engage in each activity over the course of a day, and how this schedule changes over the course of the year. Each space is tailored to a specific use and spatial quality, and the monks move from space to space as their fluctuating schedule dictates. To have a space tailored to each individual activity strikes us as somewhat extravagant today, but it raises interesting spatial issues as they relate to time. For example, what if it were the space itself that changed at different times?

In contemporary society, as urban areas become increasingly more dense, the challenge of the architect will not be to tailor the space to specific activities but to accommodate multiple activities within the same space at different times. This spatial transformation can be achieved through passive or active adaptation. The passive approach is exemplified by the Miesian notion of universal space, a space so programmatically indeterminate that almost anything can happen there. Tailored to nothing, it is noncommittal in terms of bias to any specific program. But there are limitations to this approach. While almost anything can happen in the space, almost nothing is ideally accommodated by it either. Active adaptation changes the space in a physical way to adapt to different programmatic conditions that fluctuate over time.

An example of this approach is the main practice and performance space of the Gary Comer Youth Center, which actively accommodates different programmatic conditions at different times of the day or year. Most of the time, it is a practice space for the South Shore Drill Team, the building's main user group. The space can be transformed into a theater via a motorized telescoping seating system. Doors open up to reveal a performance stage, black-out curtains deploy on three walls, and ceiling panels tilt to accommodate theater lighting. The space can also host basketball games, film screenings, lectures, and so on. By fitting these programs into one space, utilization is maximized, function is condensed, and human activity is concentrated in the heart of the building where it can permeate to the surrounding spaces.

The lineage of this approach in my work goes back through several projects that explored the notion of programmatically adaptable space. A notable early example is the Coach House, in which various programs were enclosed in furniture elements that could be deployed as circumstances dictate. A space for a missionary organization that could convert to a chapel once a week led to our first school commission, the Akiba-Schechter Jewish Day School, where space limitation on a dense urban site inspired a similar strategy.

The idea of spatial adaptation reached its apotheosis in the Perth Amboy High School project, where it operates at the scale of the entire building. The project is conceived as a civic cultural center superimposed over a high school. The school's communal spaces are arrayed across the site in towers that are contiguous with the classrooms but independent of them, allowing for use by the public when the school is closed. At certain times of the day or year, the complex functions as a high school; at other times, a cultural and recreational center for the community. The diagrams below speculate graphically about how time and space might overlap for different users throughout the day, and how this might fluctuate over the course of the year. [02]

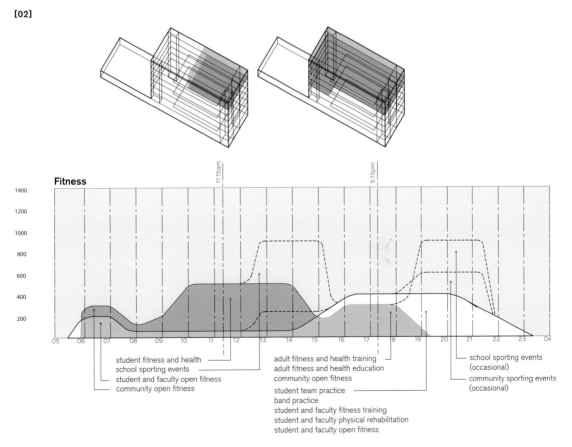

Perth Amboy High School

(2003–2004)

Perth Amboy, New Jersey

The winning entry in the Perth Amboy High School Competition, this project explores the interface between this New Jersey community and its high school and proposes a hybrid institution that functions simultaneously as school and civic cultural center. With a continuous tissue of programmatically adaptable bars, it represents the apotheosis of several of the themes explored in earlier projects.

The project foregrounds an interesting contemporary phenomenon—the way communities derive identity from their institutions and the resulting invention that takes place. The program for the school practically describes a city unto itself, and

after initial review, I realized that the project confirmed my initial impression: it held the latent possibility of the school playing a much larger role in the life of the community. Given its location on the periphery of the city, its success would depend on the extent to which it could involve this wider community. This suggested that the project should not take the form of a traditional school at all, but rather it should be a hybrid institution—part school, part cultural center.

The resulting design was not seen as a building per se but as the sum total of three superimposed systems: the natural and constructed surface of the site, which we called the *Mat*; the interconnected volumes

Early sketch over topographic plan

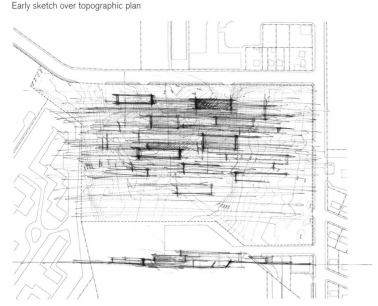

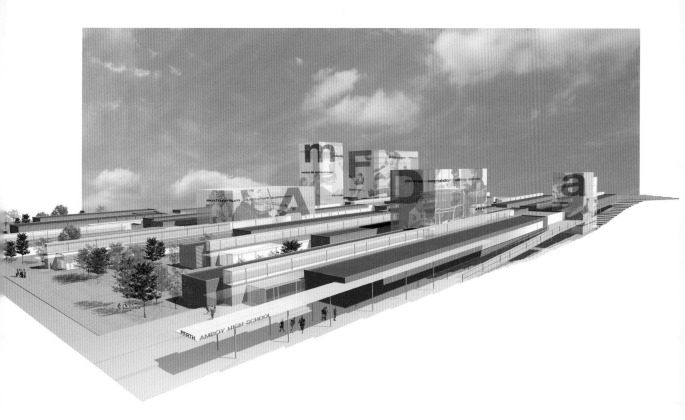

housing the programmatic requirements of the academies, called the *Barscape*; and the taller volumes housing communal programs shared by the school and the greater community, called the *Towers*. One of the competition's jury members likened the project to an organism with the towers being its vital organs.

Mat

The site's surface is constructed as a continuous mat with different programmatic zones supporting various activities of the school and community: athletics, contemplation, ecology, outdoor learning, and parking. It follows the natural topography of the site and provides access on two levels to the Learning Academies and Activity Towers. The Mat employs a composite porous paving system filled with a variety of materials—grass, clay, rubber, gravel—to create a hybrid surface that blurs the boundary between hard and soft territory and expands the programmatic potential of a surface that is typically limited to parking.

Barscape

Academic learning communities are housed in a flexible arrangement of programmatically indeterminate bars that can easily expand or adapt to meet the school's changing needs. The bars are perforated to allow light into the parking area below, and together they constitute an interdependent spatial field that prioritizes flexibility and interaction.

Towers

Communal activity spaces are organized vertically into Towers that punctuate the horizontal Barscape. These glass Towers house the spaces that are open to the greater Perth Amboy community—media center, fitness center, theater—and they also serve as visual markers linking the school to the city. The glass Towers allow visual access to the activities within and establish a connection with the community to encourage civic participation.

Early sketches

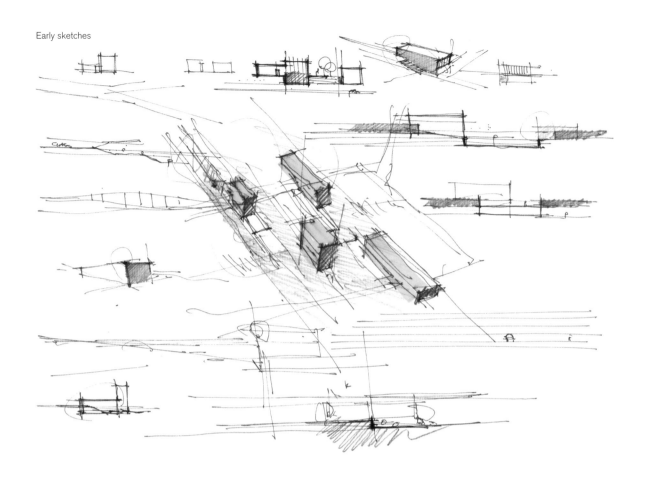

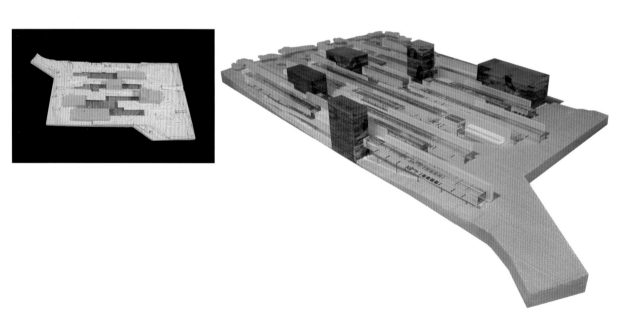

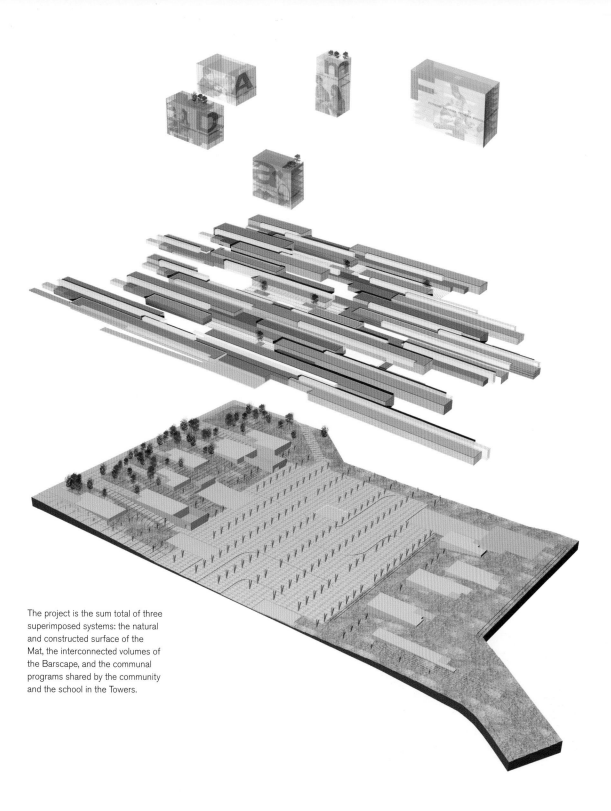

The project is the sum total of three superimposed systems: the natural and constructed surface of the Mat, the interconnected volumes of the Barscape, and the communal programs shared by the community and the school in the Towers.

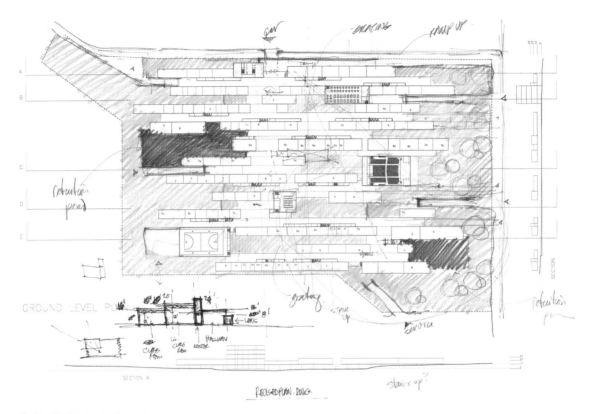

Sketch with site plan development

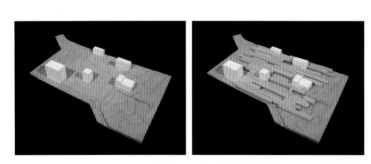

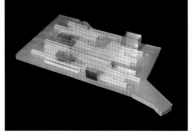

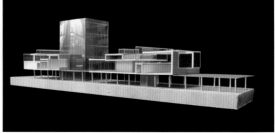

Located on the town's periphery, the project serves as an identity piece and gateway to the city.

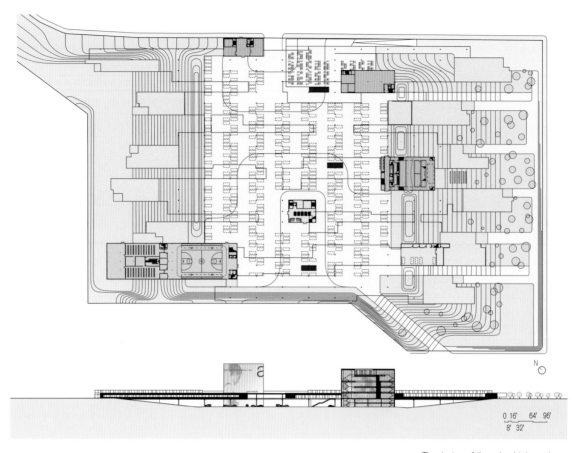

N

0 16' 64' 96'
  8' 32'

The design of the school takes advantage of the site's natural topography: low in the center and rising at either end. Parking is located on grade beneath the Barscape, which can be entered from grade at each end.

The Parking Field located beneath the academic bars employs a structural porous paving system that forms a perforated slab that can be filled with grass, gravel, rubber, or clay to code the site's surface according to program.

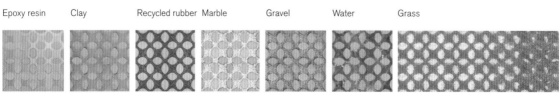

Epoxy resin   Clay   Recycled rubber   Marble   Gravel   Water   Grass

The Contemplative Field at the east end of the site is reserved for intellectual pursuits. The area is intended as a place for students to congregate alone or in groups, engage in conversation, play chess or musical instruments, or read.

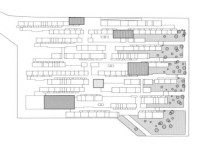

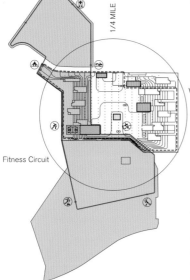

1/4 MILE

Walking Circuit

Fitness Circuit

The Athletic Field adjacent to the Fitness Tower at the west end of the site provides space for outdoor recreation and provides a link to the other athletic fields to form a contiguous athletic campus.

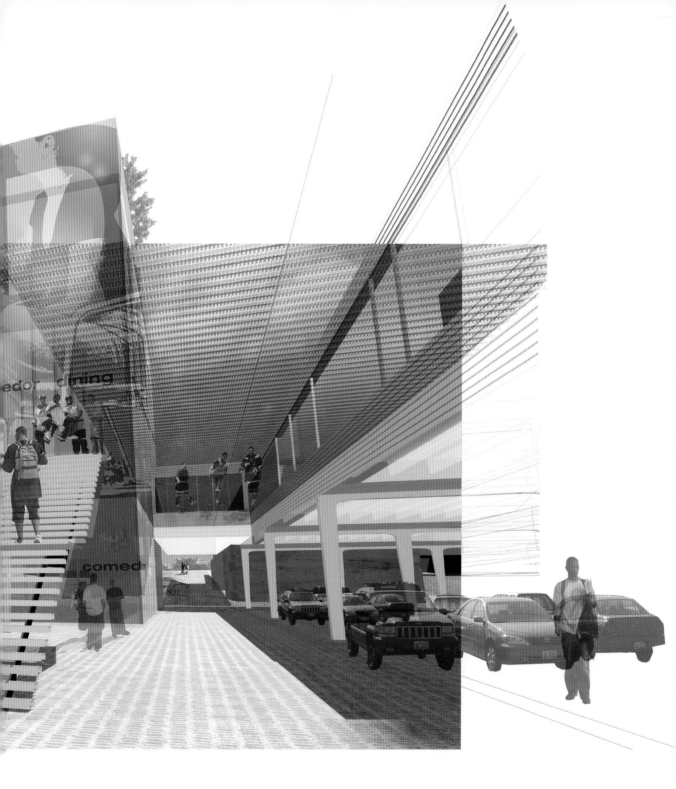

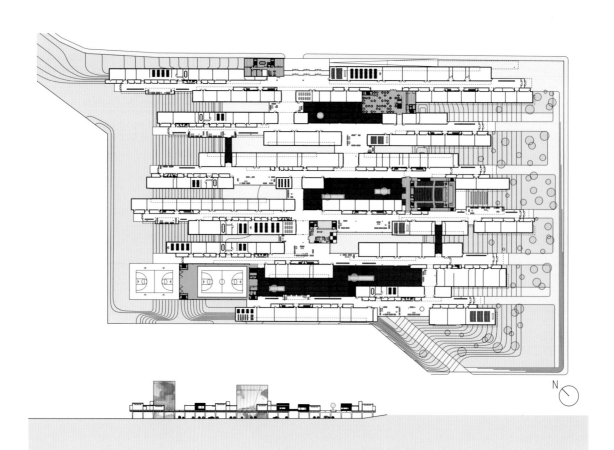

The academic bars are unrestrained
and free to expand outward.

The academies expand or adapt
internally to meet the school's
changing needs.

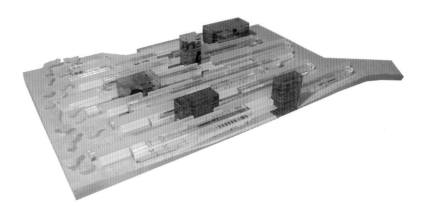

Section model through Barscape

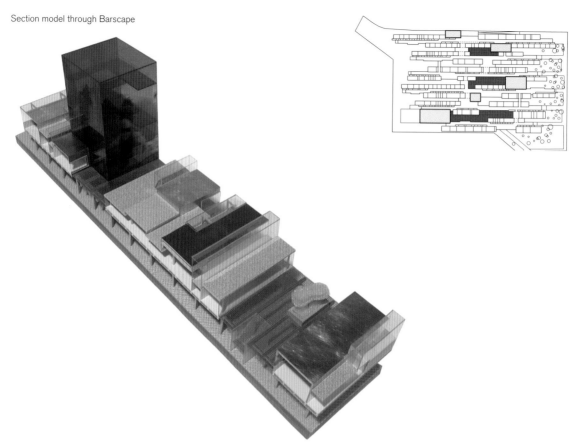

Each academy has a Commons Area that is connected with a continuous interior path linking the different academies and fostering interaction between them. Classrooms that define each particular academy are located along this path to cultivate an awareness of the unique opportunities each academy has to offer.

Entry courtyards provide supervised access from the Parking Field below and are multifunctional in that they serve as outdoor classrooms or social gathering spaces for events held in the auditorium, gym, or dining hall.

The floor surface of the courtyards is perforated-steel planking to allow light and air into the on-grade parking area below.

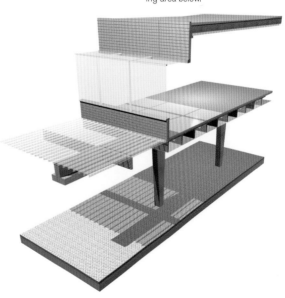

Partial building section through main
entry and courtyard

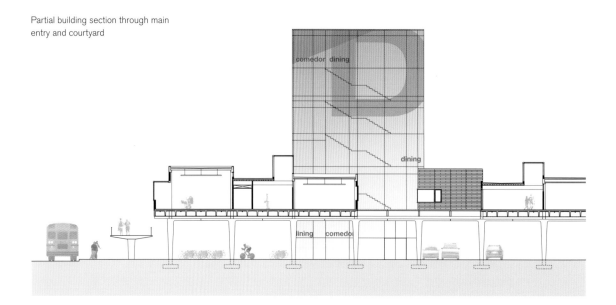

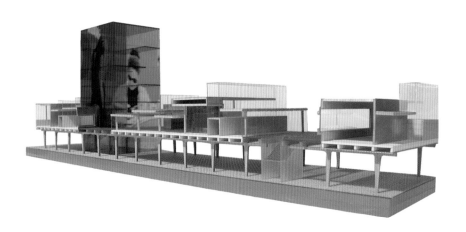

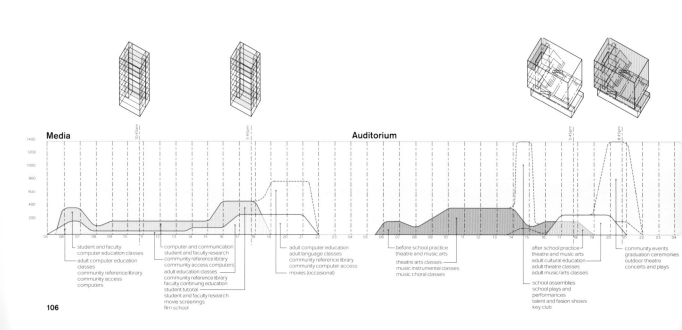

Media

Auditorium

student and faculty
computer education classes

adult computer education
classes
community reference library
community access
computers

computer and communication
student and faculty research
community reference library
community access computers

adult education classes
community reference library
faculty continuing education
student tutorial
student and faculty research
movie screenings
film school

adult computer education
adult language classes
community reference library
community computer access

movies (occasional)

before school practice
theatre and music arts

theatre arts classes
music instrumental classes
music choral classes

school assemblies
school plays and
performances
talent and fasion shows
key club

after school practice
theatre and music arts
adult cultural education
adult theatre classes
adult music/arts classes

community events
graduation ceremonies
outdoor theatre
concerts and plays

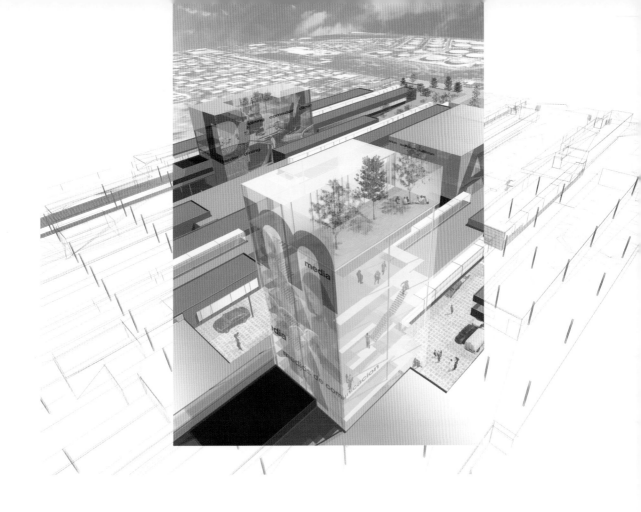

Diagram of time-based activities in
the Towers by user group

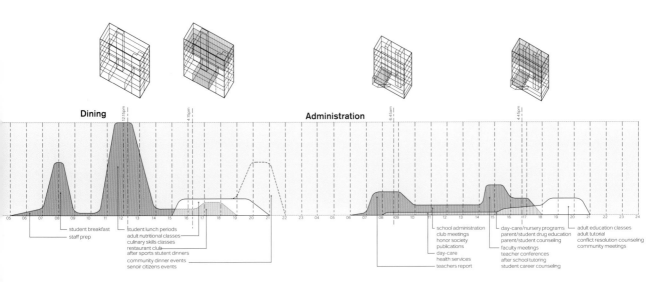

Dining   **Administration**

12.15pm   4.15pm   6.45am   4.45pm

student breakfast	school administration
staff prep	club meetings
student lunch periods	honor society
adult nutritional classes	publications
culinary skills classes	day-care
restaurant club	health services
after sports student dinners	teachers report
community dinner events	
senior citizens events	

day-care/nursery programs — adult education classes
parent/student drug education — adult tutorial
parent/student counseling — conflict resolution counseling
faculty meetings — community meetings
teacher conferences
after school tutoring
student career counseling

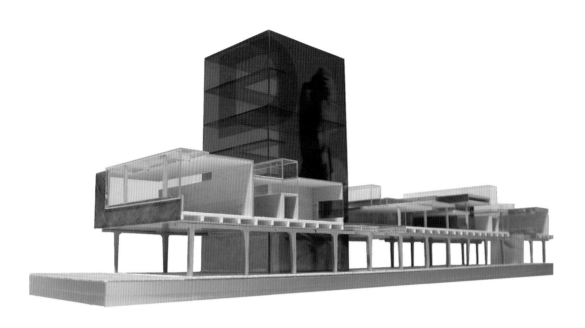

The Towers are seamlessly integrated into the academy Barscape at the main level but can be directly accessed from the Parking Field for community events and programs.

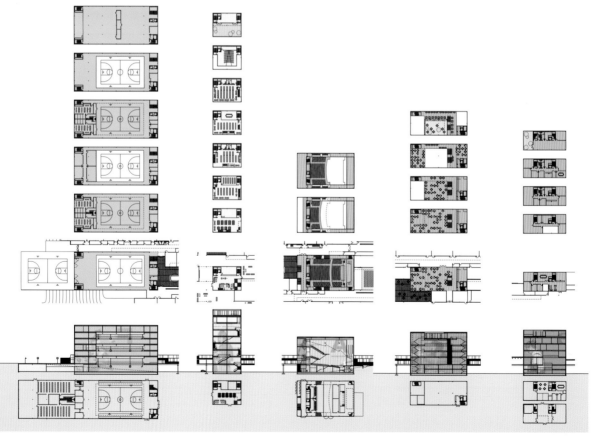

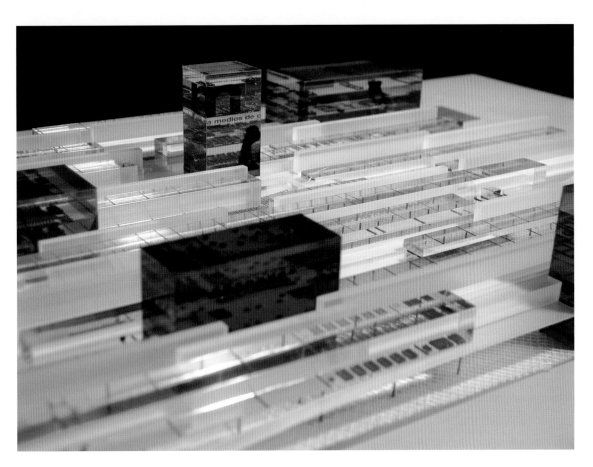

Tinted glass cladding and coded graphics allow visual access to the activities within and establish a programmatic identity for the school.

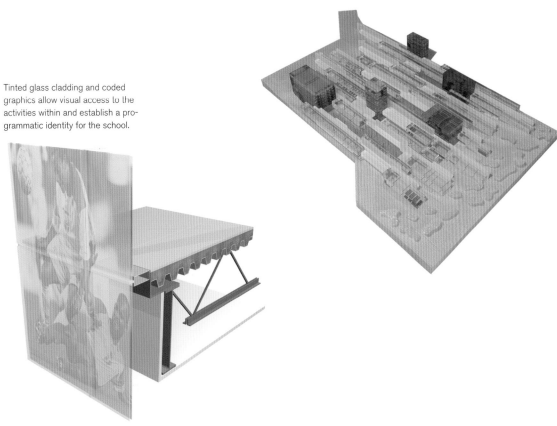

The Old Post Office

(2003)

Chicago, Illinois

In the autumn of 2003 the Chicago Central Area Committee with the help of architect Stanley Tigerman commissioned a study focusing on several persistent design problems within the city. One of them was a question about what to do with the Old Post Office, a 2.7-million-square-foot structure built in 1921 that had fallen into disuse. The building's robust structure alludes to its former role as a distribution hub and temporary storage facility for Chicago's many catalog companies, including Sears and Montgomery Ward.

The Old Post Office project proposes converting the extant structure into an urban burial site for the people of Chicago. The city devotes over 78 million square feet of land to cemeteries that are becoming increasingly overcrowded. Approximately 24,000 people die in Chicago each year, and by 2060 this figure is projected to be 36,000 people per year. As the city grows denser and land pressures increase, we will be forced to rethink how we remember our fellow citizens.

This project envisions how a new and unique burial ritual could begin to make use of the adjacent Chicago River. Funeral barges float silently down the river to where the Old Post Office once stood. A landing at the river's edge leads up an incline to the building's large, rusting steel doors. The doors open to reveal a long hall lined on one side with funeral chapels. The rear walls of the chapels allow access to the

Chicago Post Office, shortly after completion, by Graham, Anderson, Probst & White, 1921

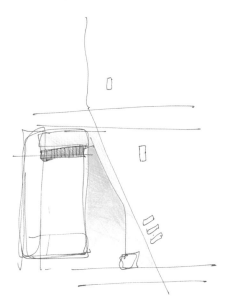

Sketch of river landing and ramped walkway

crypts above, where funeral processions wind past glass reliquaries that hold souvenirs of lives now past. The reflections of candle flames flicker in the polished floor, animated by the wind passing through the open facade.

Light and air enter the crypt through the open-air metal facade, whose patterned repetition references the hivelike workspaces of the adjacent Loop business district. Placed over the rear of the existing building, this new facade allows for vertical expansion and serves to reorient the building toward the river. Rusting COR-TEN steel cladding is proposed for the existing highway tunnel that cuts through the building, punctuating the moment of crossing the threshold of the Loop.

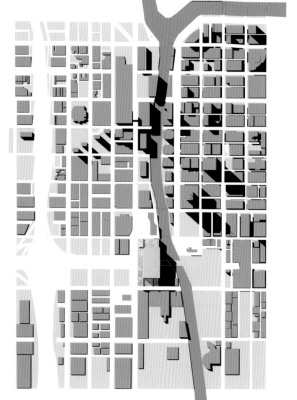

Vicinity plan

Aerial site rendering

A funeral barge on the
Chicago River

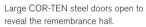

Large COR-TEN steel doors open to
reveal the remembrance hall.

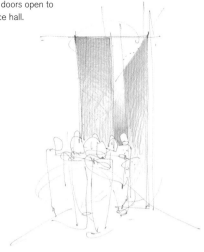

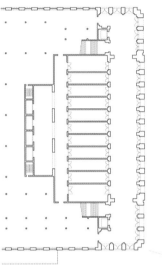

Funeral chapels line one side of the
remembrance hall.

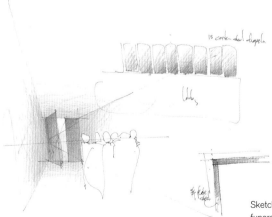

Sketch of mourners exiting the
funeral chapel

The dead are entombed in niches and crypts numbering 90,000 per floor.

Sketch of mourners walking up to the crypt

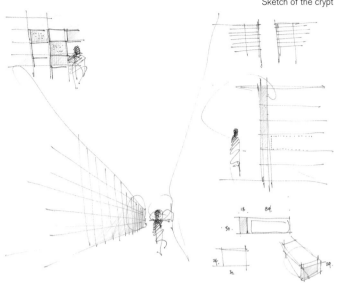

Crypts are stacked six high and consist of a fiber-reinforced casing with an ornamental stone plaque bearing the individual's name. Outside of the plaque is a glass reliquary where mementos of the deceased are preserved for posterity. Small cylindrical holes in the floor provide space for visitors to leave votive candles.

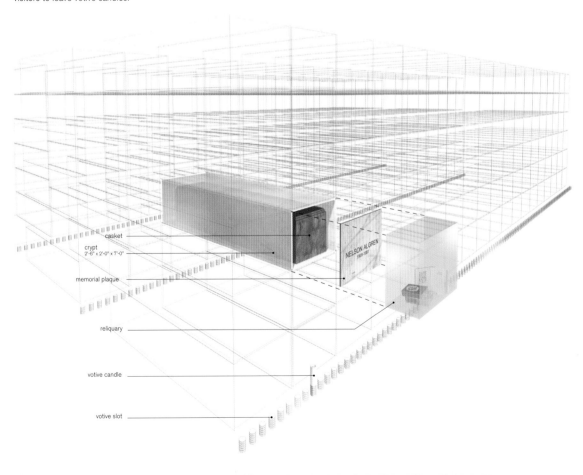

casket

crypt
2'-6" x 2'-0" x 7'-0"

memorial plaque

reliquary

votive candle

votive slot

NELSON ALGREN
1909-1981

When viewed frontally, the glass
wall speaks to the individual niche;
viewed obliquely, it dissolves into a
single reflective plane.

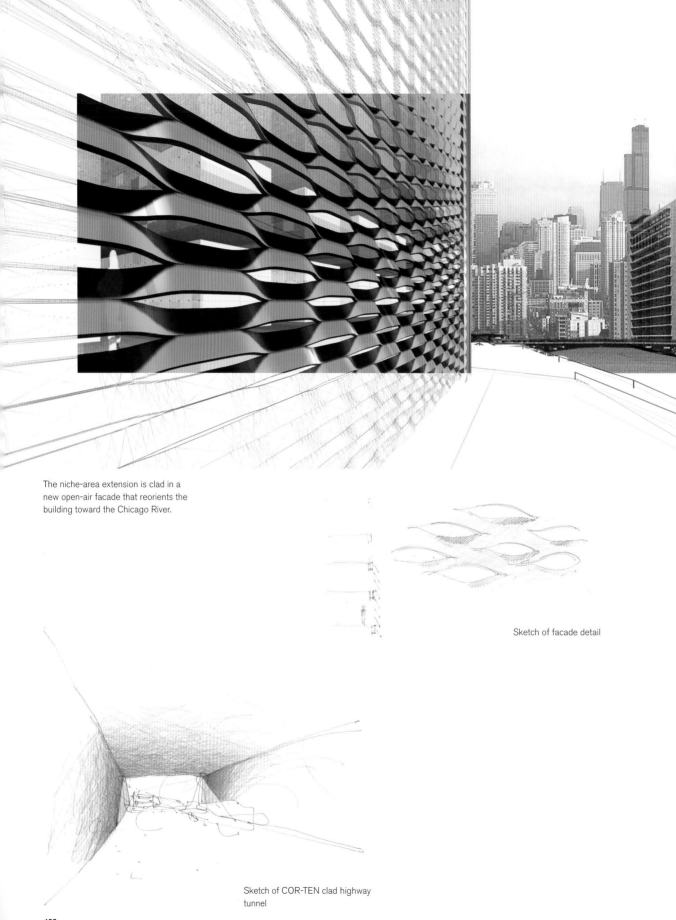

The niche-area extension is clad in a
new open-air facade that reorients the
building toward the Chicago River.

Sketch of facade detail

Sketch of COR-TEN clad highway
tunnel

House on the Lake

(2004)

St. Joseph, Michigan

This house on Lake Michigan mediates between two site conditions, an urban street on one side and a sand dune and beach on the other. The narrow site becomes progressively longer each year due to sand that piles up against a pier constructed in the 1960s to the south of the site. The house's attenuated shape reflects this reality and also references the form of driftwood sticks that wash up on its beach.

The project consists of three elements: an indoor lap pool, the main house, and the guesthouse over the garage. The overall form of the structure is inflected to take advantage of the views of the lighthouse to the south.

Materials were chosen carefully to respond to the local environment, where winds originating from the west travel unimpeded over the lake to produce hot, breezy summers and windy, frigid winters. Copper cladding on the walls and roof will react with the moist air to create an uneven patinated surface over time. Teak on the exterior walls and deck will take on a sandblasted finish over time, as windblown sand pelts the building. Travertine slabs clad the exterior terraces and continue into the house and pool.

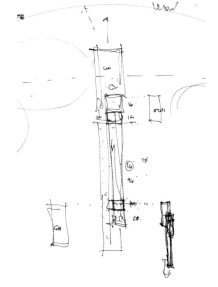

Early site sketch

Site photos in winter (left) and summer

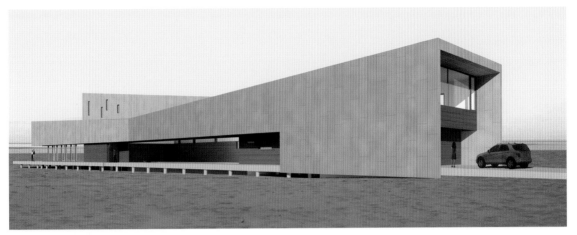

The house inflects toward a lighthouse
located south of the site.

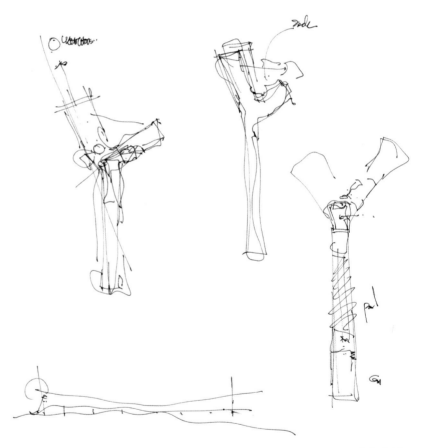

Early sketches

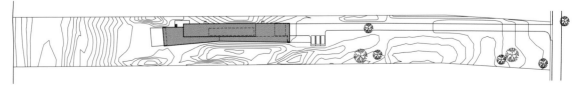

Site plan

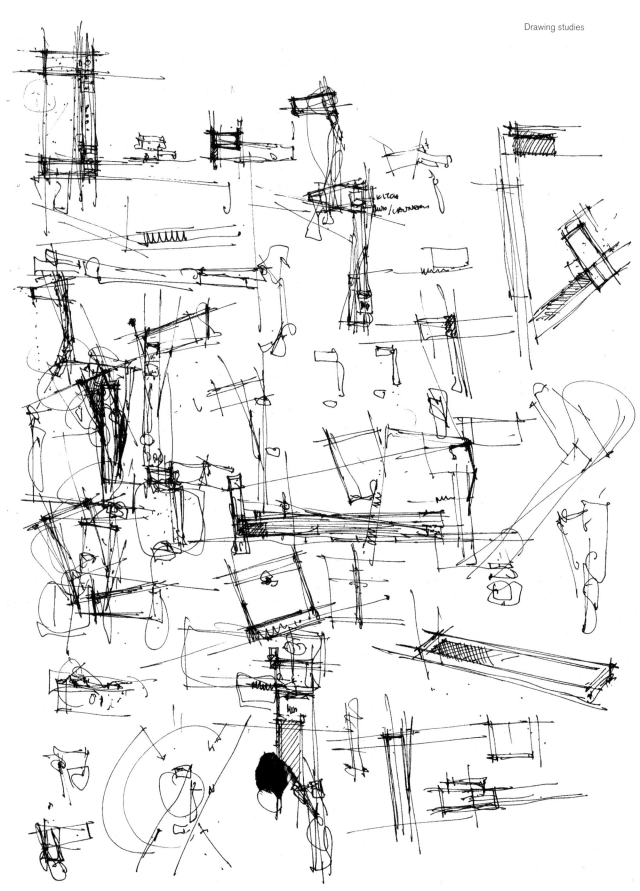

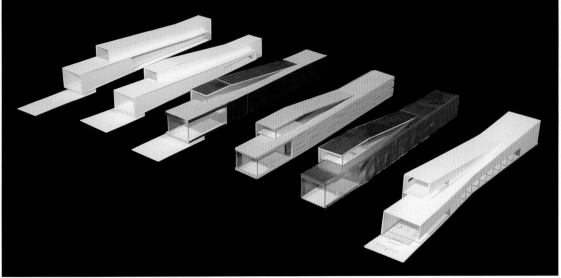

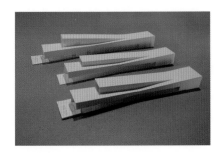

The house increases in volume as it approaches the west to take advantage of views to the lake.

Second-floor plan

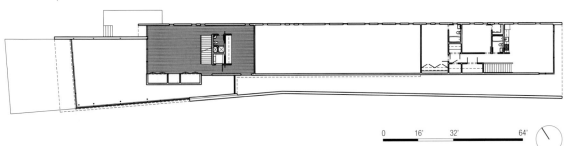

0   16'   32'   64'

First-floor plan

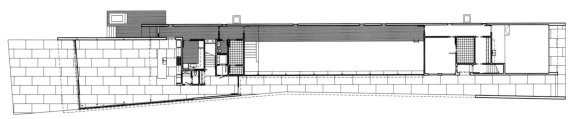

South elevation

North elevation

Street elevation (left) and beach
elevation

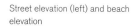 

Gary Comer Youth Center

(2004–2006)

Grand Crossing neighborhood, Chicago, Illinois

Located on Chicago's South Side, the Gary Comer Youth Center supports the activities of the South Shore Drill Team and provides a wide range of educational and recreational programs to young people after hours. It was realized by Gary Comer, who grew up in the community and went on to found the Lands' End clothing company. After returning to his old neighborhood and seeing it in need, he stepped in to bring positive change to the community. The youth center is the centerpiece of this effort.

Though originally envisioned as a practice space for the South Shore Drill Team (a successful performance troupe), the building program was ultimately expanded to include a wide variety of activities, from gardening to music recording. While the drill team's needs were understood and quantifiable, other programs were constantly in flux throughout design and construction. This condition of programmatic fluidity resulted in an organizational strategy of centering the larger, more programmatically defined spaces and wrapping them with bars of adaptable space.

The building's primary programs are concentrated into one main practice space that converts to a 600-seat performance venue via a series of motorized deployments: a theater seating system emerges from under the lobby, wall panels open to reveal a large stage, ceiling panels tilt open to uncover stage lighting, and

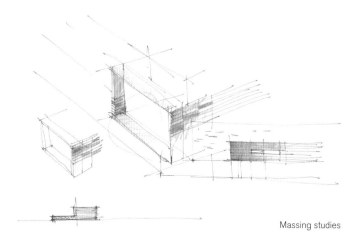

Massing studies

Early study models

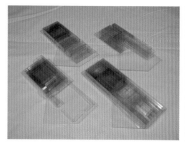 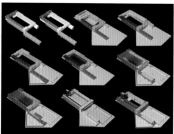 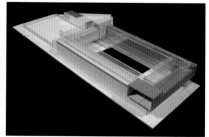

theater curtains lower to black out the space and improve the room's acoustics. Together with the adjacent cafeteria, the practice and performance space is the focal point of the complex. Bars of flexible space for educational and recreational programs wrap around this core and terminate in the dance and art rooms, which are expressed on the building's exterior, displaying the center's activities to the community.

Classrooms and exhibition spaces on the third floor overlook a large roof garden that is situated over the assembly spaces. The garden serves as an outdoor horticultural classroom, where children can grow and harvest crops for the culinary arts program. Skylights in the roof landscape bring natural light into the gym and cafeteria below.

On the exterior, the programs wrapping the main spaces are legible as four interlaced bars, clad in metal and fiber-cement panels that are colored in a seemingly random pattern that speaks to the center's youthful orientation. A mesh tower surmounted by an LED sign announces programs and events and serves as a landmark for the newly revived neighborhood.

Site plan

Early sketch of the space
in performance mode

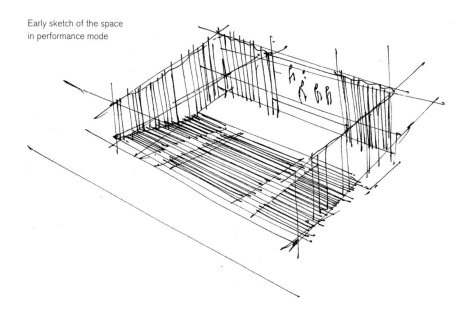

Lower-level plan

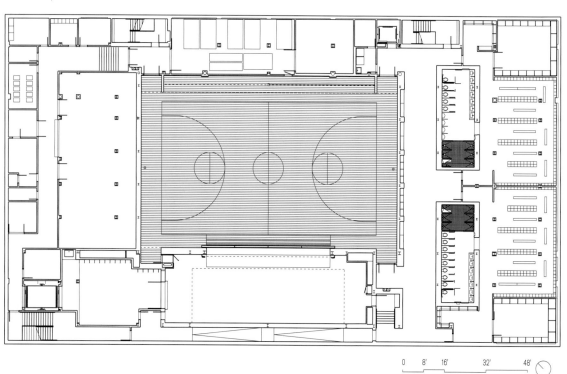

0   8'   16'   32'   48'

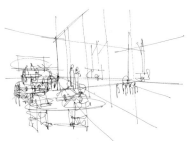

Early sketch of cafeteria/gym
interface

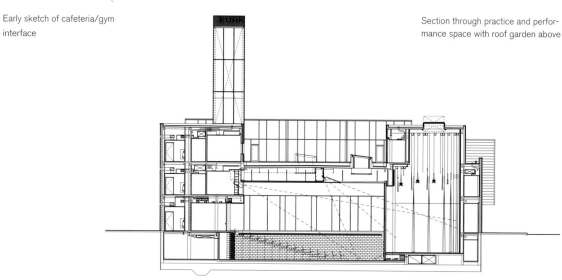

Section through practice and performance space with roof garden above

Ground-floor plan with the main
space in performance mode

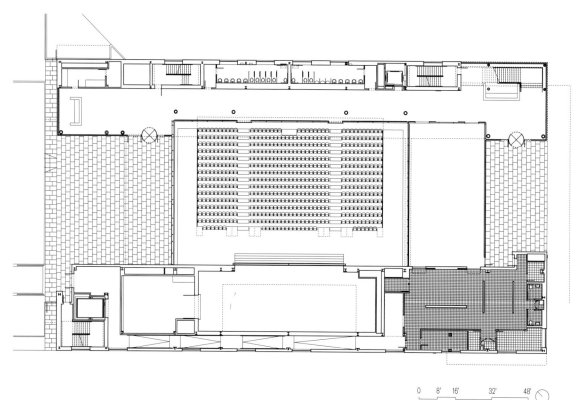

0   8'   16'   32'   48'

Second-floor plan

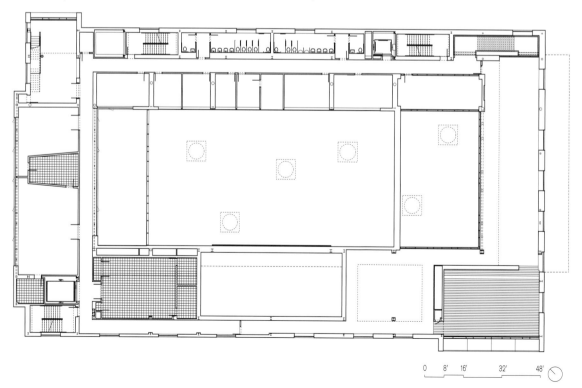

0 8' 16' 32' 48'

Programmatic bars terminate in important spaces—such as the dance room—on the building's exterior to advertise the activity inside to the community.

Early concept sketches for roof
garden and gym ceiling

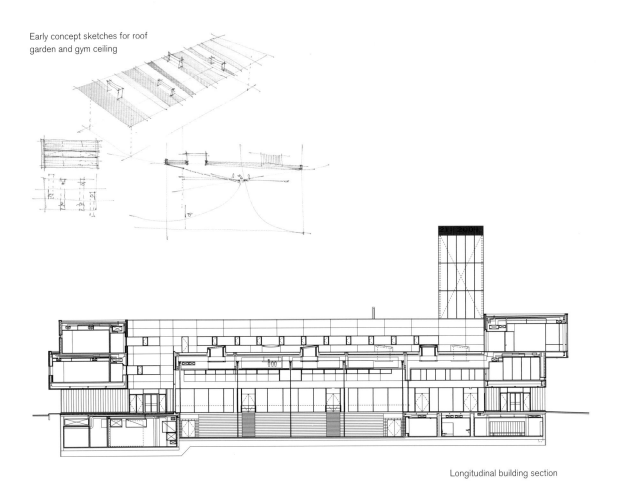

Longitudinal building section

Third-floor plan with roof garden

0   8'   16'   32'   48'

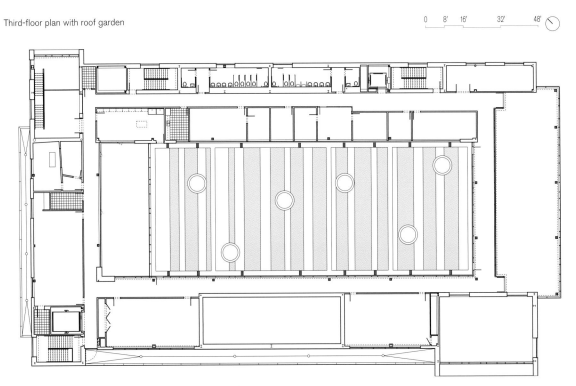

The roof garden is planted with two feet of soil to allow for a wide range of plantings, from vegetables to flowers and grasses.

A large, flexible exhibition space looks out over the roof garden. It can be blacked out for lectures or subdivided into seminar rooms.

On the third level, the programmatic
bars wrap around a large roof garden
that is divided into bands of plantings.
Glass divisions correlate with the
bands for plant identification.

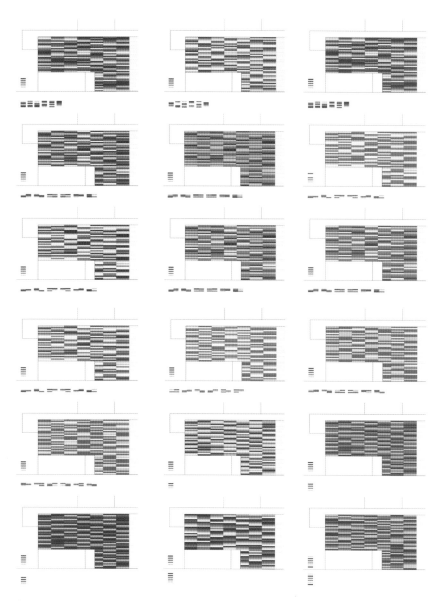

Cladding panel permutations

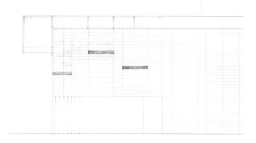

Facade study

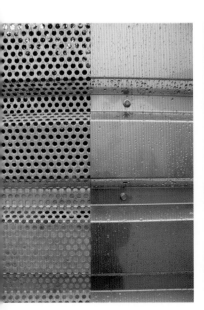

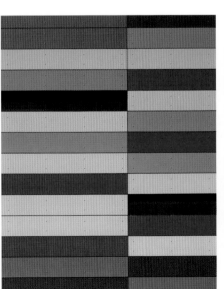

[01A–C]

Impermanence

Several years ago the Illinois Institute of Technology announced plans to restore Mies van der Rohe's Crown Hall (where I teach). In anticipation of the project, I began to take notice of the current state of the physical structure and document the character that it had acquired. [01A-E] Over time it had taken on a sad beauty. The steel on the stairs was disintegrating. Materials that were once discrete and separate were now melding together as rust migrated from the steel to the adjacent concrete, commingling in ways never intended by Mies. Cracks in the translucent glass were indifferent to the architecture's otherwise rigid geometry. Weather stains on the steel had begun to differentiate one bay from the next, disallowing their uniformity, while wavy reflections in the terrazzo floor refuted claims of flat perfection. The building had grown imperfect through use, and nature was conspiring against it. To my eyes, the structure had grown more interesting, but this acquired character contradicted our collective perceptions of Crown Hall and its allusion to Cartesian perfection. This would all be erased in the subsequent restoration for the sake of reestablishing our historical perceptions. The "real" Crown Hall—its complicated physical history—was eventually expunged, removed from our consciousness.

Memory, however, is not easily erased. The pre-restoration Crown Hall that I had photographed continues to teach us a lesson about authenticity. Silently advocating for an architecture of realism, it suggests that we begin to look at the way things really are and understand that nothing is permanent, nothing is finished, nothing is ever perfect.

I believe that impermanence is the fundamental condition in which the architect now operates. A building is a temporary proposition whose destiny—driven by forces over which we have little control—is erasure, revision, or decay. Crown Hall escapes this condition because of its cultural prominence, but it is a rare case. What is called for today is a mode of operation that acknowledges the temporary condition of our built environment and embraces changes to it.

Nothing is finished. The architect operates within a continuum without beginning or end; buildings are not fixed realities, but physical conditions in a continual state of flux. The restored Crown Hall is a mere snapshot of a moment that will gradually give way to a new physical reality and a potentially new programmatic condition. Architecture, today, should concede to this and anticipate how buildings will be adapted, extended, or internally divided and likewise pursue strategies that exploit their reuse and modification. More attention should be paid to how buildings change physically over their life spans. Like a wooden bowl that acquires its beauty through use, a building should age and weather in interesting ways. The Japanese have a term for this: *wabi sabi.*

Nothing is perfect. I concluded from observing Crown Hall in the years prior to its restoration that the building's material character resided, in fact, in its imperfection rather than in the precision that its reputation had been predicated on. I began to see imperfection in a new way, cultivating an awareness of the small details that expose the physical history of the built world and engaging in the idea of imperfection, not as something to be overcome but as a point of departure for material investigation.

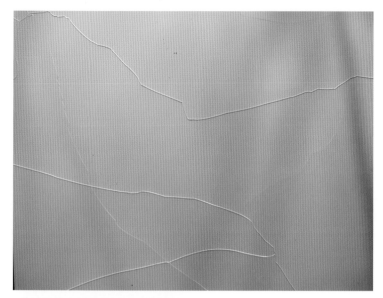

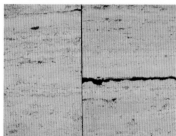

Yale Steam Laundry

(2005–2008)

Washington, D.C.

The subject of this project was a commercial laundry facility in Washington, D.C. that we were asked to renovate and transform into condominiums and amenities. The existing structure had a rich physical history written into its vaulted ceiling, oddly spaced floor framing, and pockmarked concrete and brick walls. Time had conferred upon the space a character that was worth preserving. We therefore proposed that new interventions be minimal, legible, and discrete.

Our strategy was to call attention to imperfections and frame these moments in a way that would cultivate an awareness of the past. We decided not to erase the building's history as we had done in the Coach House project a few years earlier. Instead we chose to expose it and add layers to it. To communicate these concepts to the builder, whose team was accustomed to doing patch and repair work, we conducted a rigorous review of the existing structure, documenting its surfaces to describe what was to be exposed, cleaned, or left untouched.

For the layers, we pursued a strategy of select intervention, carefully adding layers that were legible but consistent with the existing structure. In the private units, insertions were made of wood; in public spaces, glass and plate steel were employed. Welding residue and fabrication marks on the steel were left exposed to make this history visible.

Concept rendering

Physical history of the existing
structure

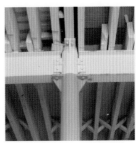

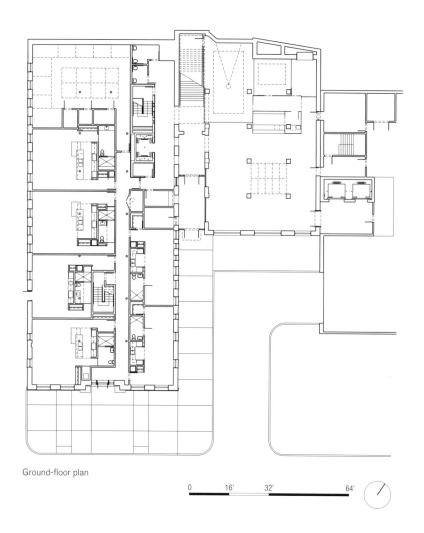

Ground-floor plan

0   16'   32'   64'

Second-floor plan

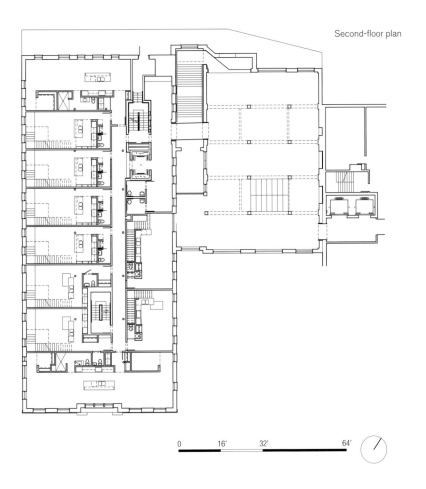

0   16'   32'   64'

A new glass bridge insertion and
skylight allows for views of the
existing smokestack.

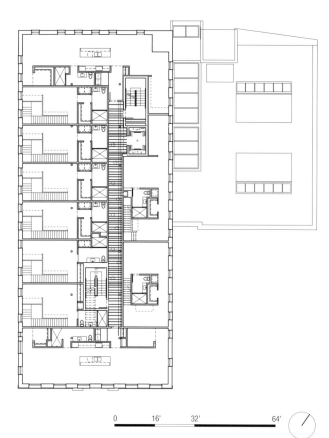

Third-floor plan with roof of the annex

0   16'   32'   64'

Minimal kitchen and bath insertions
expose the building's physical history.

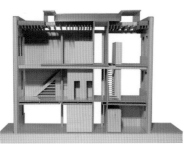

Roof plan with pool area

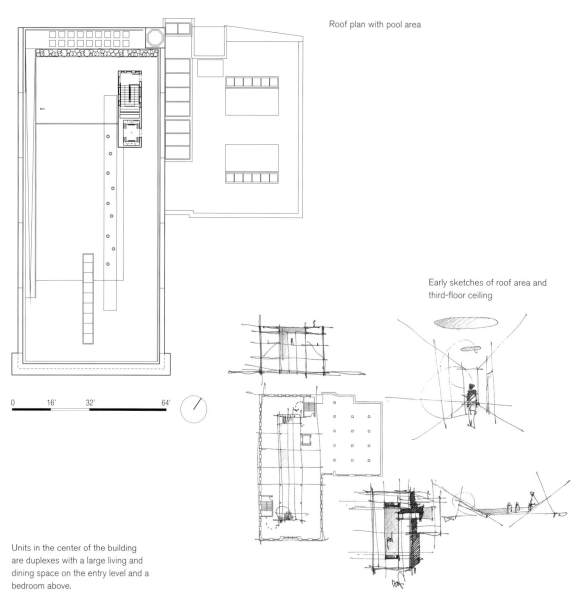

Early sketches of roof area and
third-floor ceiling

Units in the center of the building
are duplexes with a large living and
dining space on the entry level and a
bedroom above.

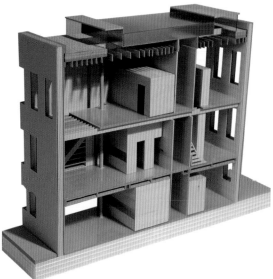

0   16'   32'   64'

Stair and elevator towers penetrate the rooftop pool. Together with the brick chimney, they form a roofscape backdrop for outdoor relaxation and private parties.

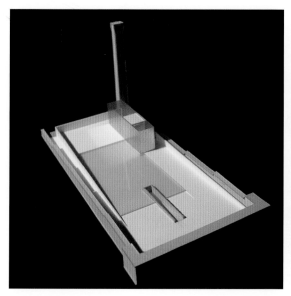

Urban Model High School

(2007–2010)

Chicago, Illinois

The Public Building Commission of Chicago asked us to design a new prototype high school for the city. Its recently completed high schools were sprawling complexes, spanning multiple city blocks, and expensive in terms of site expenditures such as land costs and utility relocations. It desired a more compact model that would fit 1,200 students within a single city block measuring 266 by 600 feet. The spatial program for each school had to be similar to maintain parity between communities, but each would have a unique identity.

We proposed a model school organized around three thematic components—body, mind, and spirit—as they relate to the city's curriculum. The site is zoned accordingly, with separate bars to house the athletics facilities (body), classrooms (mind), and library, art studios, and music rooms (spirit). These bars slide against each other to create the exterior spaces: an entry courtyard, recreation fields, and the Reading Garden.

As in other projects, adaptability and public interface are stressed. The gymnasium converts to a 1,200-seat auditorium; an adjacent space accommodates music recitals, art exhibitions, dance studios, and lectures. We proposed that some parts of the building remain open to the community to promote interaction and maximize public investment. Thus the library can be entered directly through the Reading Garden during after-school hours; likewise, the pool and gymnasium also have separate entrances.

The school is organized around three thematic bars—body, mind, and spirit—that slide against each other to create spaces for entry, contemplation, and recreation.

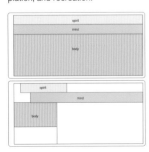

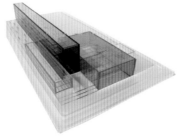

View of site plan with imposed thematic bars

Extending from the library is a walled Reading Garden that provides a quiet, contemplative space to read or engage in conversation. This space also serves as the community's entrance to the library.

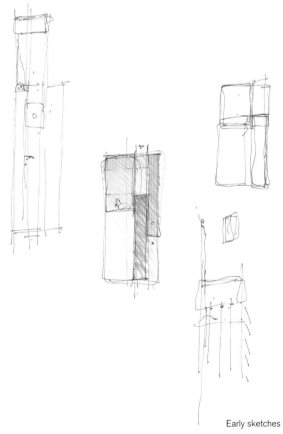

Early sketches

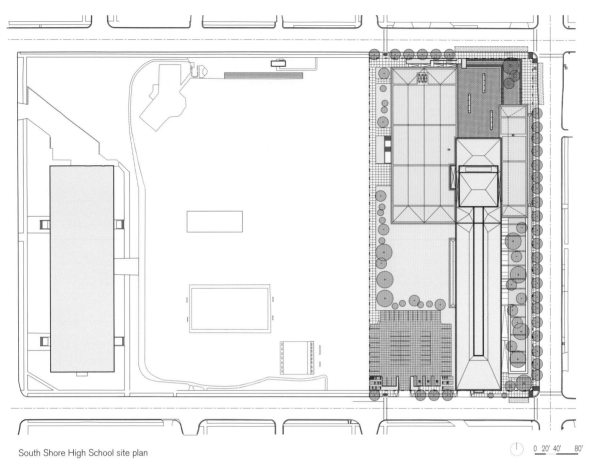

South Shore High School site plan

0 20' 40' 80'

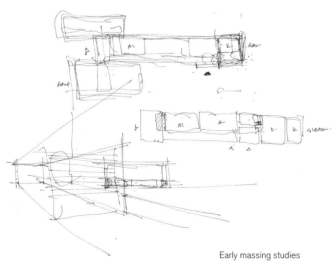

Early massing studies

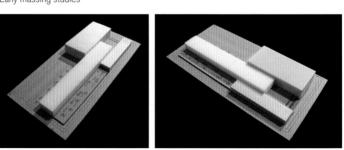

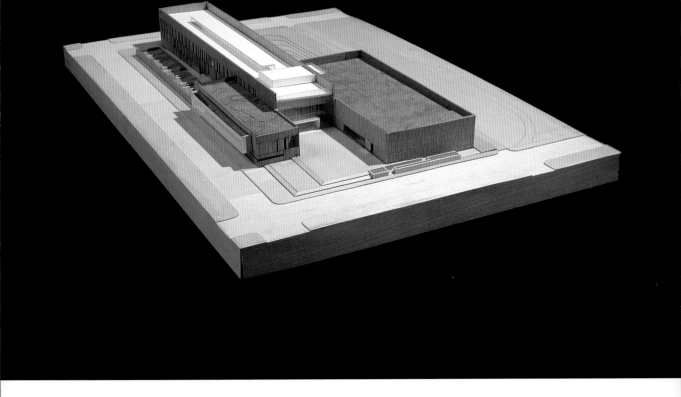

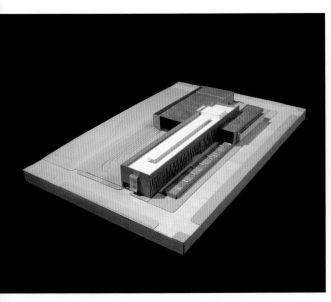
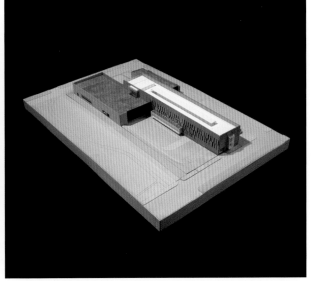

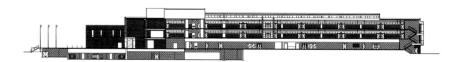

Longitudinal section through the
entry courtyard and commons area

West and north elevations

East and south elevations

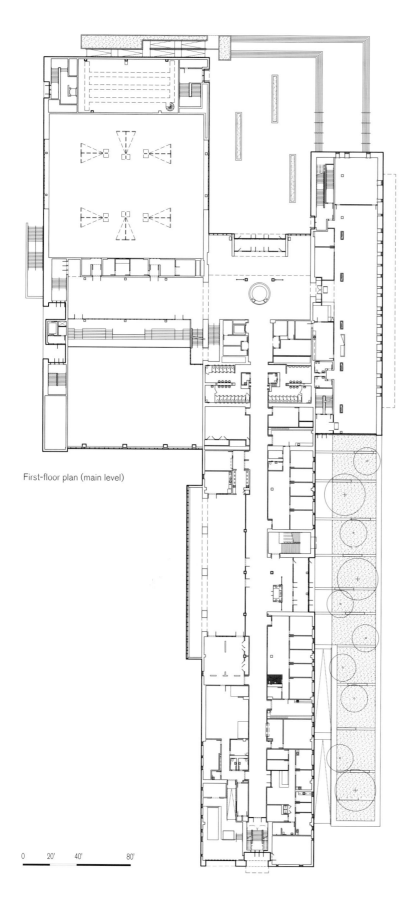

First-floor plan (main level)

0   20'   40'   80'

The academy bar slides back to create an entry courtyard between the arts and athletics volumes to form the main entrance to the building.

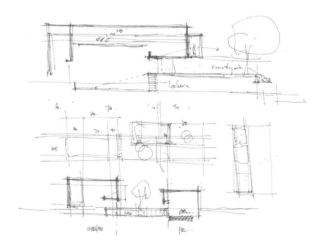

Early sketches

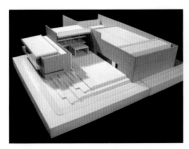

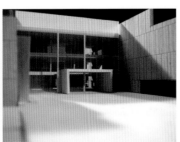

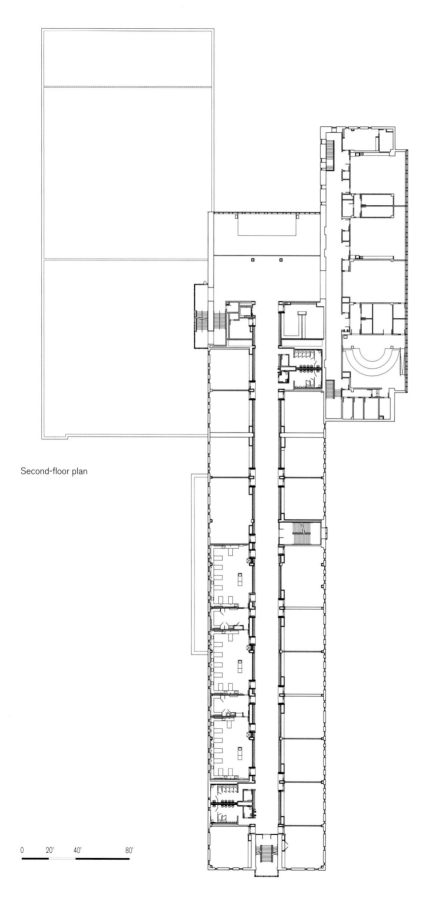

Second-floor plan

0 20' 40'   80'

The academic bar is subdivided into two academies of 600 students. Each academy has a commons area that links the two floors and overlooks the main entry.

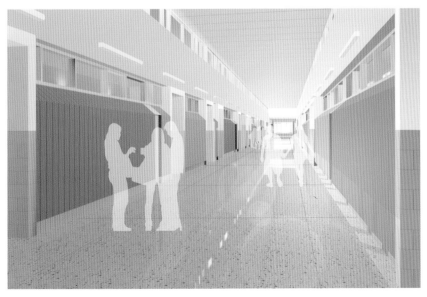

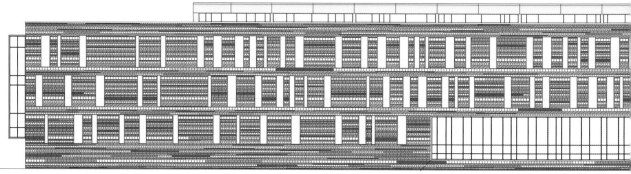

West elevation

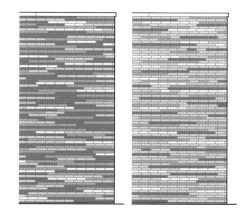

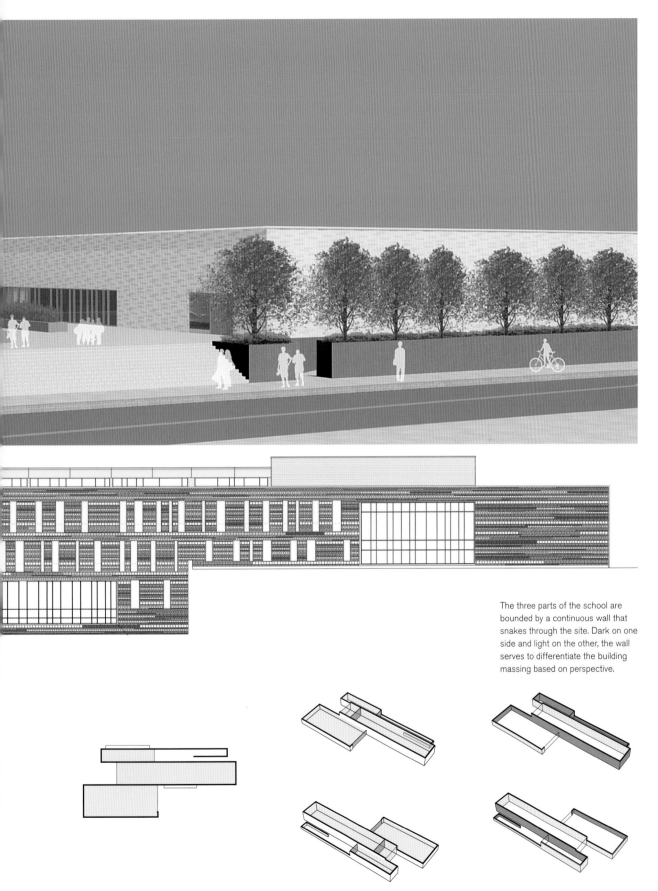

The three parts of the school are bounded by a continuous wall that snakes through the site. Dark on one side and light on the other, the wall serves to differentiate the building massing based on perspective.

Poetry Foundation

(2007–2010)

River North neighborhood, Chicago, Illinois

In the fall of 2007 we were asked to design a new home for the Poetry Foundation, a not-for-profit organization and offshoot of *Poetry* magazine dedicated to celebrating poetry in contemporary culture. The foundation had located a site, in the River North neighborhood of Chicago, that was larger than required for their proposed building, with the intent of incorporating a garden in some way. One design challenge was to find the right balance between the building's role as a home of poetry, open to the public, while providing a private space for the foundation's offices and collections.

The design process started with a series of diagrams describing possible relationships between building and garden: interlocking, overlapping, eroding, perforating, fragmenting, knotting, etc. These strategies were then applied to the site in a series of sketches and models. From these, five approaches were selected for further development. Eventually we settled on a scheme in which the garden seems to be created by forces of erosion acting on the implied volume of the property. The result is a relationship whereby the building pushes into the garden and vice versa. Visitors reach the building by walking through the garden, while the internal arrangement is configured to allow for views into the garden from all spaces.

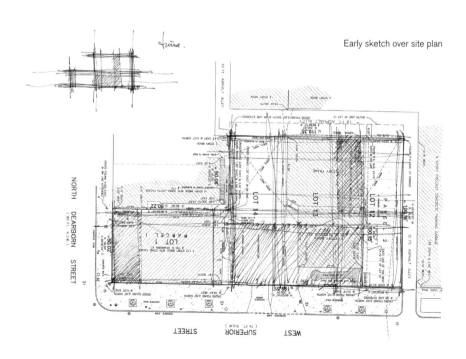

Early sketch over site plan

The garden is conceived as an urban sanctuary, a space that mediates between the street and the building and dissolves the distinction between public and private. Public spaces—a poetry reading room, gallery, and library—are located on the building's ground floor. Offices for the organization are located on the second level in three areas corresponding to operations: foundation administration, magazine and website staff, and programs staff. Upon entering the garden, visitors perceive the bordering double-height library space, which announces the entrance into a literary environment. On the interior an exhibition gallery connects the library to the reading room, where poets present their work.

Tectonically the building is conceived as a series of layers that visitors move through and between. Layers of zinc, glass, and wood peel back like pages of a book to define various programmatic zones. The building's outer layer—clad in oxidized zinc—becomes perforated where it borders the garden, allowing visual access from the street to encourage public investigation.

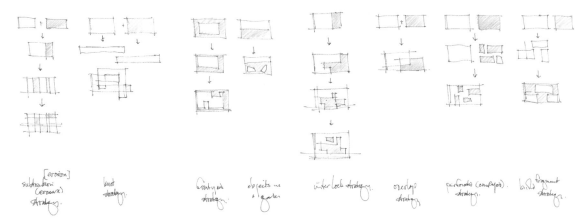

Building versus garden relational
studies

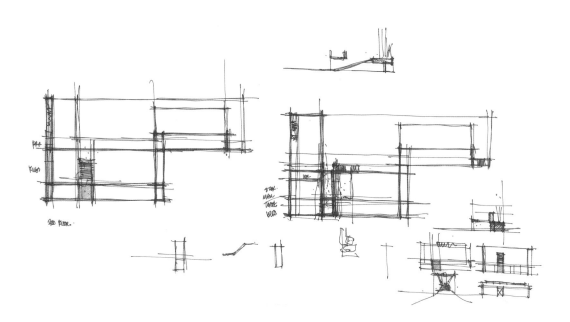

Site-specific study models of
building and garden strategies

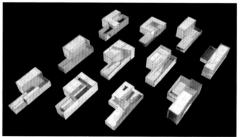
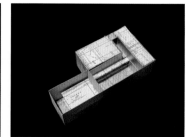

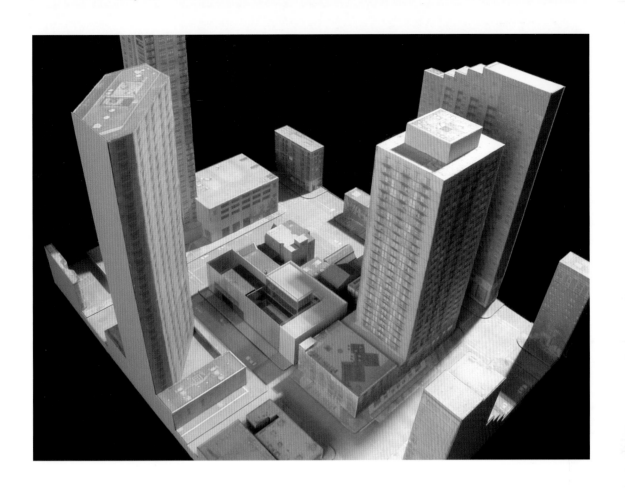

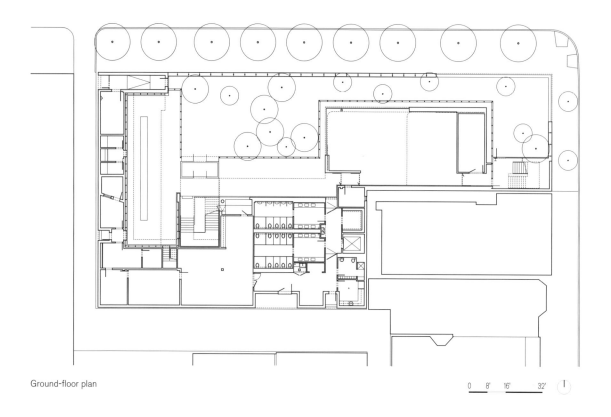

Ground-floor plan

0   8'   16'   32'

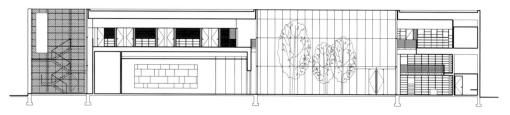

Building section through garden

The building is clad in oxidized zinc, which forms a screenwall that defines the interface between street and garden. Layers of metal, glass, and wood organize the interior spaces and orient them toward the garden.

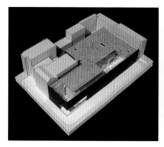
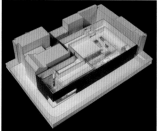

The building is accessed through an exterior garden that is screened from the street. The double-height library comes into view first.

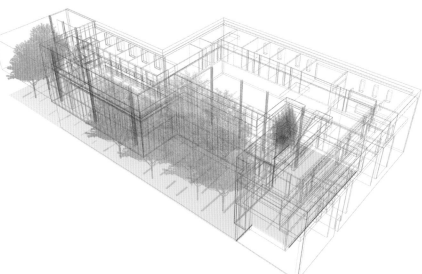

Garden surface diagram

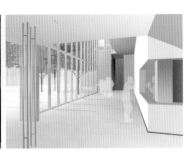

A continuous ribbon of wood shelving lines the library and second floor and terminates in the reading room at the building's east end, where poets read their work aloud.

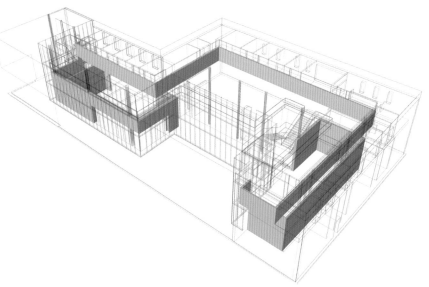

On the first floor the continuous wood shelving separates the public spaces from the nonpublic spaces. On the second floor it separates the enclosed private offices from the open-office work area.

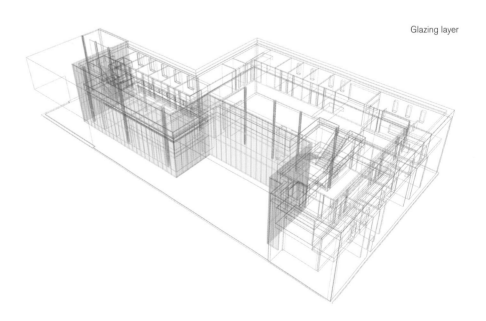

Glazing layer

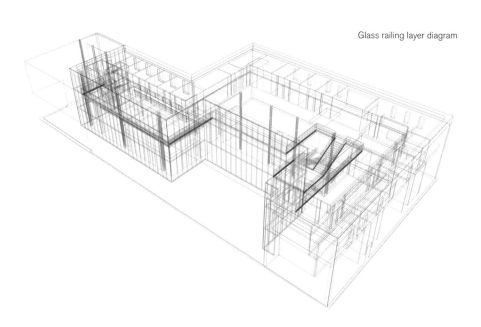

Glass railing layer diagram

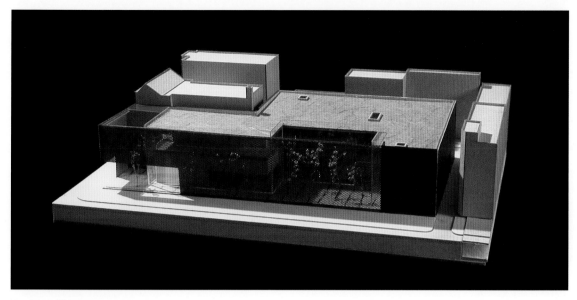

The zinc cladding becomes perforated at the garden, allowing views into the garden from the street.

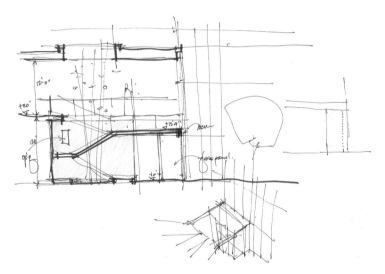

Sketch of main stair area

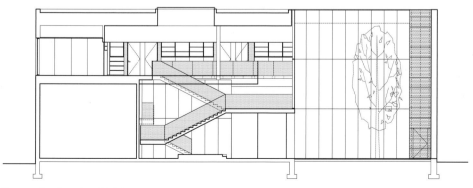

Cross section through main stair and garden

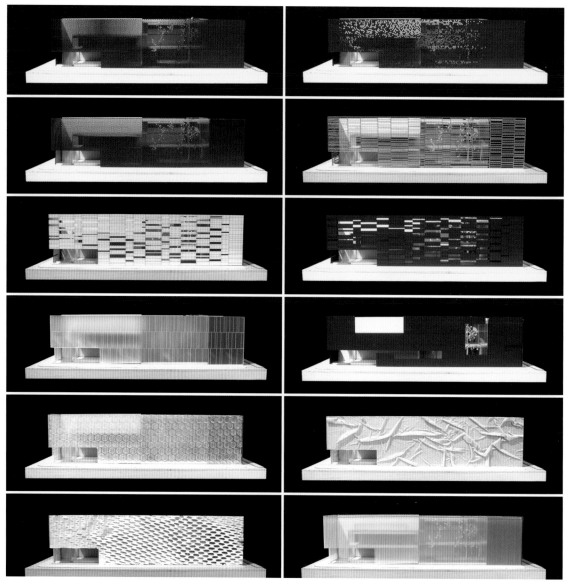

Early screenwall studies

At night the garden lighting converts
the screenwall to a thin urban veil.

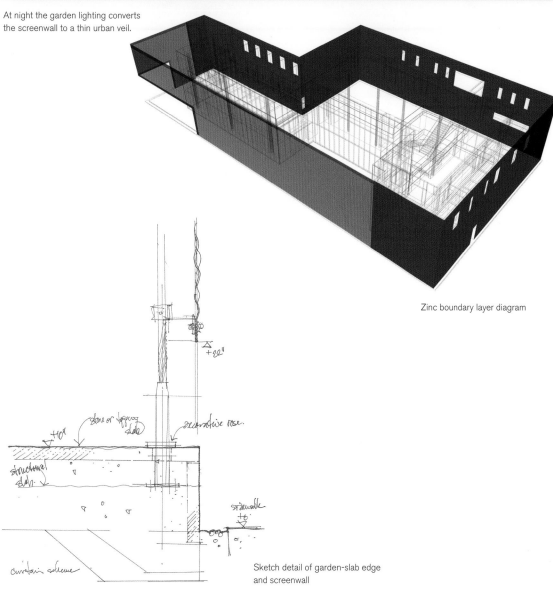

Zinc boundary layer diagram

Sketch detail of garden-slab edge
and screenwall

Acknowledgments

I admire anyone who undertakes a building project; buildings are costly investments, and even the simplest of projects is a complicated endeavor, requiring optimism, faith, and bravery. Nevertheless, the rewards are great. I would like to start by thanking the clients I have worked with over the last ten years, as I was getting my practice started. Hiring a young architect is not an easy decision, and I would like to recognize those individuals who chose to work with me when there was not a long track record to support their decision, nor, in some cases, a completed building to point to. I thank them for their courage and trust.

Over the years, I have been fortunate to have many talented and thoughtful people to work with. This book stands as a testament to their hard work and dedication, and I owe them my sincerest thanks.

I am honored to have Toshiko Mori write the foreword to this book. Her work as a practitioner and educator has served as a model for many within the architecture profession, and her groundbreaking contributions in the area of material investigation continue to inspire. Bob McAnulty was an obvious choice to conduct the interview portion of this book, for his knowledge of contemporary architecture, his perceptive observations, and his gift for trenchant questioning. My friend and colleague Brad Lynch always brings a unique and thoughtful perspective to any discussion on architecture, and I thank him for his essay, though, I suspect that I may now owe him several cases of Huber Beer for his contribution.

I would like to recognize the Graham Foundation for Advanced Studies in the Fine Arts for its generous support of this book, and I would like to thank Kevin Lippert of Princeton Architectural Press for his support of my work and for assigning first-rate editors and designers to the book's realization. I offer special thanks to Laurie Manfra at Princeton Architectural Press, whose guidance and discernment have made the book stronger, and the process of creating it smooth and enjoyable. I would also like to extend my appreciation and respect for Jan Haux, the book's designer. Assembling, editing, and formatting the material for a project like this is an enormous task, and I would like to specifically recognize those members of my studio who were instrumental in this endeavor: Tom Lee, John Trocke, Sam Zeller, and Ed Blumer.

Most of all, I would like to thank my wife Clare for her support and insight throughout the course of this project, when she had more than enough work of her own.
—John Ronan

Chronology

1999
The office of John Ronan Architects formed
Adjunct professor, Illinois Institute of Technology College of
    Architecture
209 East Lake Shore Drive

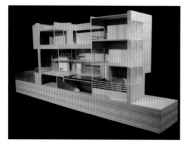

Winner, Townhouse Revisited Competition, sponsored by the Graham
    Foundation for Advanced Studies in the Fine Arts
Townhouse Revisited exhibition, Graham Foundation, Chicago, Illinois
Townhouse Revisited exhibition, School of Architecture, University of
    Illinois Urbana-Champaign, Champaign, Illinois

2000
Coach House
11 Woodley Road
513 North Walcott
428 West Webster

Redsquared
Chapel in the Woods
Catholic Extension Chapel
Chicago Architecture Club Members Show, I space Gallery, Chicago,
    Illinois
"Impermanence," published in the *Chicago Architectural Journal 9:
    Positions in Architecture* (January 2000): 100–101.

2001
Todd Hase showroom
House on the Edge of a Forest
541 West Belden
Chicago Public Schools Competition
Honorable Mention, Redsquared project, *ID* Annual Design Awards
Chicago Architecture Club Members Show, I space Gallery,
    Chicago, Illinois

2002
Catfish Music
Tiffiny Decorating Co.
ING Trading Office
Lecture: Illinois Institute of Technology College of Architecture,
    Chicago, Illinois
"Contingency," published in the *Chicago Architectural Club Journal:
    Influence Across Fields* 10 (December 2002): 100–101.

2003
Assistant professor, Illinois Institute of Technology College of
    Architecture, Chicago, Illinois
Akiba-Schechter Jewish Day School, phase I
Sabbia jewelry store
67 East Bellevue
Precast Concrete, affordable housing project
Precast Chapel, speculative project
Perth Amboy High School, winning competition entry
The Old Post Office, for Visionary Chicago Architecture project
    by the Chicago Central Area Committee
Speculative Chicago: A Compendium of Architectural Innovation,
    Gallery 400, Chicago, Illinois
Lectures: Archeworks, Chicago, Illinois; and School of Architecture,
    University of Illinois Urbana-Champaign, Champaign, Illinois

2004
House on the Lake
Winner, Perth Amboy High School Design Competition
Perth Amboy High School Design Competition exhibition,
    Architectural League of New York, New York,
Chicago Green, a companion exhibition to Big & Green: Toward
    Sustainable Architecture in the 21st Century, Chicago
    Architecture Foundation, Chicago, Illinois
Visionary Chicago Architecture: Fourteen Inspired Projects for the
    Third Millennia exhibition, Graham Foundation, Chicago, Illinois

2005
Long Bay Villas, Anguilla
Chicago Line Vessel
South Chicago Avenue streetscape

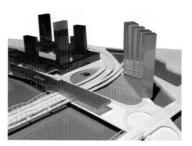

Chicago Square, master plan, HafenCity, Hamburg, Germany
Distinguished Building Award, House on the Edge of a Forest,
    AIA Chicago
Interior Architecture Award, Coach House, AIA Chicago

Citation, Perth Amboy High School, 52nd Annual P/A Awards
52nd Annual P/A Awards Exhibition, Center for Architecture, New
    York, New York
Lectures: Emerging Voices, Architectural League of New York, New
    York, New York; Auburn University Rural Studio, Newbern,
    Alabama; Graham Foundation for the Advancement of the
    Fine Arts, Chicago, Illinois; Catholic University of America,
    Washington, D.C.; and the University of Wisconsin-Milwaukee,
    Milwaukee, Wisconsin

2006
Akiba-Schechter Jewish Day School, phase two II
Concrete Townhouse
Gary Comer Youth Center
3020 Lake Shore Drive
Herman Miller Classics project
First Place, Gary Comer Youth Center, Richard H. Driehaus
    Foundation Award for Architectural Excellence in
    Community Design
Winner, GreenWorks Award from the City of Chicago,
    Gary Comer Youth Center
Young Chicago exhibition, Art Institute of Chicago, Chicago, Illinois
Perth Amboy High School Design Competition exhibition, Cornell
    University College of Architecture, Art, and Planning, Ithaca,
    New York
Lecture: University of Illinois at Chicago, Chicago, Illinois

2007
South Caicos, Turks and Caicos master plan
Urban Model High School concept design
CMK Company Offices

Chicago 2016, Live Site and Archery Venue
Divine Detail Award, Distinguished Building Award, and Sustainable
    Design Award, Gary Comer Youth Center, AIA Chicago
Distinguished Building Award, Akiba-Schechter Jewish Day School,
    AIA Chicago
American Architecture Award, Gary Comer Youth Center, Chicago
    Athenaeum Museum of Architecture and Design
First Place, Gary Comer Youth Center, Chicago Building Congress
    Merit Awards
Lectures: University of Tennessee, Knoxville, Tennessee; McGill
    University, Montreal, Quebec, Canada

2008
Associate professor, Illinois Institute of Technology College of
    Architecture
Yale Steam Laundry
House for Two Artists
Lock Rum Villas, Anguilla
South Caicos Villas, Turks and Caicos
South Caicos Check-in and Beach Club, Turks and Caicos
Unbuilt Design Award, the Old Post Office, AIA Chicago

2009
Kelly Curie Gage Park High School, under construction
South Shore High School, under construction
Courtyard House
Desert House
Poetry Foundation

Christ the King Jesuit College Preparatory School,
    under construction

House in Three Parts

Gary Comer College Prep, under construction
National Honor Award, Gary Comer Youth Center,
    American Institute of Architects
Award of Excellence, Green Roofs for Healthy Cities,
    Gary Comer Youth Center

Selected Bibliography

2009

Achilles, Rolf. "Hamburg's five-sided Square." *Chicago Architect*, May/
June 2009, 36–39.

"AIA Honor Awards." *Architectural Record*, May 2009, 118.

Coleman, Cindy. "Subtraction = Addition." *Chicago Architect*, Jan/
Feb 2009, 27.

2008

Brown, Lara. "John Ronan Ponders Designing a Home for Verse."
Chicago Architect, March/April 2008, 9–10.

Coleman, Cindy. "Superb Reduction." *Interior Design*, October 2008,
69–72.

Gonchar, Joann. "John Ronan's Bright and Bold Gary Comer Youth
Center Supports an Ambitious Agenda on Chicago's South
Side," *Architectural Record*, February 2008, 114–9.

Kamin, Blair. "City Taps Top Architects for Prototype Revision.
Chicago Tribune, August 31, 2008.

Killory, Christine and René Davids. *Detail in Process*. As Built 2. New
York: Princeton Architectural Press, 2008.

Phaidon Atlas of 21st Century World Architecture. London: Phaidon
Press, 2008.

2007

Amadei, Gian Luca. "Chicago, Reinventing a Legacy." *Blueprint*, May
2007, 68–72.

Bey, Lee. "Chicago Hope." *Architect Magazine*, March 2007, 80–85.

Kamin, Blair. "Chicagoans of the Year: Architect's Youthful Dreams
Unfold in his Mature Work." *Chicago Tribune*. December 30,
2007.

Kamin, Blair. "City's New Modern Marvels Win Top Design Awards."
Chicago Tribune, October 26, 2007.

Pridmore, Jay. "Ten Modern Masterpieces." *Chicago Magazine*,
September 2007, 88–89.

"The Gary Comer Youth Center." *Arkhitekturny Vestnik Magazine*
(Russia), no. 3 (2007): 54–59.

2006

Berreneche, Raul. "Don't Say Modern; Say Light, Air and Space." *New
York Times*, July 27, 2006.

Educational Facility. Alexandria, Australia: Archiworld Press, 2006.

Focus on HafenCity Hamburg. Hafencity Hamburg Gmbh, 2006.

Hockenberry, John. "Miracle on 72nd Street," *Metropolis*, December
2006, 89–96.

"House on the Lake." *Architectural Record web edition,* April 2006,
http://archrecord.construction.com/projects/portfolio/
archives/0604unbuilt/houseOnTheLake/overview.asp.

Kamin, Blair. "New Youth Center in Grand Crossing a Beacon of
Optimism." *Chicago Tribune*, June 4, 2006.

Ronan, John. "The Diagram." *Architectural Review*, January 2006,
64–65.

2005

Becker, Lynn. "If It Looks Like a Mausoleum…" *Chicago Reader*.
June 10, 2005.

Bey, Lee. "John Ronan Saves a Coach House from Certain Death
with a Clever Use of Light, Space and Materials." *Architectural
Record*, January 2005, 194–7.

Casas en la Ciudad. Barcelona: Insituto Monsa de Ediciones, 2005.

"Emerging Voices." *Architect's Newspaper*. March 9, 2005.

"Perth Amboy High School." *Architecture*, 2005 P/A Awards, January
2005, 38–41.

Reed, Cheryl. "Vision Quest: Top Local Architects Imagine a Cool
New Future for Chicago." *Chicago Sun-Times*. June 17, 2005.

Sirefman, Susanna. *Contemporary Guesthouse*. ed. Sarah Palmer.
Milan: Edizioni Press, 2005.

2004

Becker, Lynn. "One to Watch: A Splashy New High School Puts John
Ronan on the Map." *Chicago Reader*, March 5, 2004.

Berger, Philip. "Quality Control." *Chicago Tribune Magazine*, March
21, 2004.

Bussel, Abby. "On the Boards: Gary Comer's Youth Center."
Architecture, October 2004, 42.

Dulin, Michael. "Raising the Bar(s) in the Garden State."
Competitions, Spring 2004, 16–19.

Grossberg, Deborah. "Upset Victory in New Jersey." *Architect's
Newspaper*, March 9, 2004.

Kamin, Blair. "Chicago's Bold Rebirth." *Chicago Tribune*, April 18,
2004.

Kamin, Blair. "City Architect Scores Upset Over 3 National Rivals
for $84 Million Dollar Project." *Chicago Tribune*, February 26,
2004.

Kamin, Blair. "Ones to Watch: These Architects Are Sketching
Tomorrow's Chicago." *Chicago Tribune*. March 28, 2004.

Keegan, Edward. "Building on Tradition: John Ronan Ennobles the
Warehouse with Simple Materials and Hebrew Tradition for a
Chicago school." *Architecture*, December 2004, 84–87.

Lubell, Sam. "Ronan's Design Will Alter a Town, Not Just a School."
Architectural Record, October 2004, 38.

Walsh, John. "Ronan Raises the Bar." *New Zealand Architecture*, July/
August 2004, 32–33.

2003

Berger, Philip. "Singular Sensation." *Chicago Tribune Magazine*, July
2003, 18–21.

Bey, Lee. "An Upgrade from Coach." *Dwell*, May 2003, 31–32.

Coleman, Cindy. "Design Hits a High Note." *Interior Design Magazine*,
November 2003, 58–60.

Reed, Cheryl. "Chicago's Architectural Revival is New Stars' Chance
to Shine." *Chicago Sun-Times,* October 1, 2003.

Vincenti, Lisa, "Modern Classic," *Shelter Magazine*, December 2003,
24–27.

1999–2002

"Chicago's New Standout Architects." *CS Magazine*, September
2002, 110–11.

Hart, Sara. "John Ronan Seeks the Essence of Space in Structure
and Material." *Architectural Record,* December 2000, 42–43.

Kamin, Blair. "Young Turks Have Designs on the Townhouse of
Tomorrow." *Chicago Tribune*, April 20, 1999.

"Redsquared." *ID Magazine,* August 2001, 46.

Vincenti, Lisa. "Vanguards of Design." *Shelter Magazine*, October
2002, 25–26.

Project Credits

Coach House (1999–2000)
Location: Chicago, Illinois
Client: James and Molly Perry
Project team: John Ronan
Builder: Eiesland Builders

House on the Edge of a Forest (2000–2001)
Location: Northbrook, Illinois
Client: Margot and Daniel Kaplan
Project team: John Ronan, David Strong, Yasushi Koakutsu,
          Paul Dean
Builder: Fraser Construction

Akiba-Schechter Jewish Day School (2000–2005)
Location: Chicago, Illinois
Client: Akiba-Schechter Jewish Day School
Project team: John Ronan, Brian Malady, Yasushi Koakutsu, Sonja
          Mueller
Consultants: Robert L. Miller & Associates (structural); CCJM
          Engineers (MEPFP); Terra Engineering (civil)
Builder: The Meyne Company (phase one); Levine Builders
          (phase two)

Concrete Townhouse (2002–2004)
Location: Chicago, Illinois
Client: James and Molly Perry
Project team: John Ronan, Brad Kelley, Yasushi Koakutsu,
          Sonja Mueller
Consultants: Fraser Design Group (structural)
Builder: Fraser Construction

Precast Chapel (2003)
Project team: John Ronan, Brian Malady, Oscar Kang, Brad Kelley,
          Micah Land

Perth Amboy High School (2003–2004)
Location: Perth Amboy, New Jersey
Client: New Jersey Schools Construction Corporation
Project team: John Ronan, Brian Malady, Yasushi Koakutsu,
          Brad Kelley, Micah Land, Oscar Kang
Consultants: Arup (structural)

The Old Post Office (2003)
Location: Chicago, Illinois
Client: Chicago Central Area Committee
Project team: John Ronan, Micah Land

House on the Lake (2004)
Location: St. Joseph, Michigan
Client: Brad and Jody Kapnick
Project team: John Ronan, Oscar Kang, Yasushi Koakutsu,
          Sonja Mueller, Evan Menk, Nageshwar Rao, Micah Land
Consultants: Robert L. Miller & Associates (structural)
Builder: Lakeshore Enterprises

Gary Comer Youth Center (2004–2006)
Location: Chicago, Illinois
Client: Comer Science & Education Foundation
Project team: John Ronan, Brian Malady, Evan Menk, Brad Kelley,
          Yasushi Koakutsu, Oscar Kang, Nageshwar Rao, Micah Land
Consultants: Arup (structural); CCJM Engineers (MEPFP);
          Terra Engineering (civil); Peter Lindsay Schaudt Landscape
          Architecture (landscape); Kirkegaard Associates (acoustics);
          Shuler & Shook (theatrical); Charter Sills (lighting)
Builder: W. E. O'Neil Construction

Yale Steam Laundry (2005–2008)
Location: Washington, D.C.
Client: IBG Partners/Greenfield Partners
Project team: John Ronan, Brian Malady, Brad Kelley,
          Yasushi Koakutsu, Oscar Kang, Sonja Mueller
Consultants: BBGM (architect of record); Holbert Apple Associates
          (structural); GHT Limited (MEPFP); Charter Sills (lighting)
Builder: Clark Construction

Urban Model High School (2007–2010)
Location: Chicago, Illinois
Client: The Public Building Commission of Chicago
Project team: John Ronan, Kevin Wineinger, Evan Menk, Tom Lee,
          Sonja Mueller, John Trocke, Anna Ninoyu, Sam Zeller,
          Andrew Smith, Yujin Park
Consultants: Rubinos & Mesia Engineers (structural); Environmental
          Systems Design (MEPFP); Prism Engineering (civil);
          Terry Guen Design Associates (landscape); Kirkegaard
          Associates (acoustics); Edge Associates (food service);
          Bill Connor Associates (theater); Innovative Aquatic Design
          (pool); Charter Sills (lighting)
Builder: F. H. Paschen Construction (Kelly Curie Gage Park Area
          High School); The George Sollitt Construction Company
          (South Shore High School)

Poetry Foundation (2007–2010)
Location: Chicago, Illinois
Client: The Poetry Foundation
Project team: John Ronan, Tom Lee, John Trocke, Evan Menk,
          Wonwoo Park
Consultants: Arup (structural); dbHMS (MEPFP); Terra Engineering
          (civil); Reed/Hilderbrand (landscape); Threshold Acoustics
          (acoustics); Sako Associates (security); Anders Dahlgren
          (library); Charter Sills (lighting)
Builder: Norcon Construction

Photo Credits

All photographs, drawings, and renderings courtesy of John Ronan Architects unless otherwise noted

Contingency
p. 22 top left: reproduced by permission of the syndics of Cambridge University Library; p. 25 bottom: Yasushi Koakutsu

Coach House
pp. 26 middle left, 27 top left, 28 top left, 31, 32–34, 36 bottom, and 37 top: Nathan Kirkman

House on the Edge of a Forest
pp. 39 top and bottom left, 40–41, 42 top, bottom center, and bottom right, 44 bottom left and bottom right, 45 top, and 47: Steve Hall; p. 45 bottom left: Nathan Kirkman; p. 38 bottom right: Yasushi Koakutsu

Akiba-Schechter Jewish Day School
pp. 48 bottom right, 49 top, 55 top and bottom left, and 60–61: Steve Hall; pp. 50–51, 54 bottom left and bottom right, 55 bottom right, 56, and 57: Nathan Kirkman; p. 59 bottom: Yasushi Koakutsu

Concrete Townhouse
pp. 62 bottom left, 63, 64, 65 top, 68 bottom left and bottom right, 69 bottom left and bottom center, 70 middle left and middle right, 71, and 75: Steve Hall

Precast Chapel
pp. 83 bottom left and bottom right, 86 bottom left and bottom right, and 87 bottom left: Oscar Kang

Adaptation
pp. 88 and 91: diagrams redrawn by John Ronan Architects, based on images appearing on p. 56 of *Cistercian Abbeys: History and Architecture* by Jean-Francois Leroux-Dhuys and Henri Gaud (Konigswinter, Germany: h.f. ullman, 2008)

Perth Amboy High School
pp. 94 bottom right, 103 top left and bottom right, 104 top left, 106 middle left, 108 top, and 109 top and middle right: Yasushi Koakutsu

The Old Post Office
p. 110 bottom left: photographer unknown

House on the Lake
p. 125 top, middle, and bottom left: Yasushi Koakutsu

Gary Comer Youth Center
pp. 131 top, 132 bottom left and bottom right, 133, 134 top, bottom center, and bottom right, 135, 137 top and bottom, 139 top, 140 top left and top right, 141 top and bottom left, 143 top left, bottom center, and bottom right, 144, 145 top, and 147 top, bottom center, and bottom right: Steve Hall; pp. 139 bottom left, bottom center, and bottom right, and 141 bottom center: Chris Lake

Yale Steam Laundry
pp. 160 bottom left and 161 bottom left: Oscar Kang; pp. 153 top left, 154 bottom center and bottom right, 155 top, bottom left, and bottom right, 156 top, bottom left, and bottom right, 157 bottom left and bottom right, 158 bottom left, bottom center, and bottom right, 159 top and bottom left, and 161 bottom right: Nathan Kirkman

Urban Model High School
pp. 162 bottom center, 164 bottom center and bottom right, 165 top, bottom left, and bottom right, and 169 bottom left and bottom center: Andrew Smith

Poetry Foundation
pp. 176 bottom center and 177 top, bottom left, and bottom right: Tom Lee; pp. 178 bottom center and bottom right, 183 top, and 184 top and bottom: John Trocke; p. 176 bottom right: Sam Zeller